LEADING WOMEN

Entrepreneur and First Daughter

Ivanka Trump

MEGAN MILLS HOFFMAN

New York

Published in 2018 by Cavendish Square Publishing, LLC
243 5th Avenue, Suite 136, New York, NY 10016

First Edition

Library of Congress Cataloging-in-Publication Data

Names: Hoffman, Megan Mills.
Title: Ivanka Trump : entrepreneur and First Daughter / Megan Mills Hoffman.
Description: New York : Cavendish Square, 2018. | Series: Leading women | Includes index.
Identifiers: ISBN 9781502627018 (library bound)ISBN 9781502627025 (ebook)
Subjects: LCSH: Businesswomen--United States--Biography--Juvenile literature. |
Trump, Ivanka,--1981-.
Classification: LCC HC102.5.A2 H727 2018 | DDC 658.4'0092'273--dc23

Editorial Director: David McNamara
Editor: Tracey Maciejewski
Associate Art Director: Amy Greenan
Designer: Lindsey Auten
Production Coordinator: Karol Szymczuk
Photo Research: J8 Media

The photographs in this book are used by permission and through the courtesy of: Cover Dimitrios Kambouris/Getty Images for Lincoln Center for the Performing Arts; p. 1 John Lamparski/WireImage/Getty Images; p. 4 Taylor Hill/FilmMagic/Getty Images; p. 7 The LIFE Picture Collection/Getty Images; p. 18 Pierre Vauthey/Sygma/Sygma via Getty Images; p. 22 Jon Kopaloff/FilmMagic/Getty Images; p. 30 Mathew Imaging/FilmMagic/Getty Images; p. 36 Brian Marcus/Fred Marcus Photography via Getty Images; p. 41 Joe Raedle/Getty Images; p. 46 George Pimentel/WireImage for The Bay/Getty Images; p. 56 Amanda Rivkin/AFP/Getty Images; p. 60 Philip Ramey/Corbis via Getty Images; p. 72 MANDEL NGAN/AFP/Getty Images; p. 74 Andrew Harrer/Bloomberg via Getty Images.

Printed in the United States of America

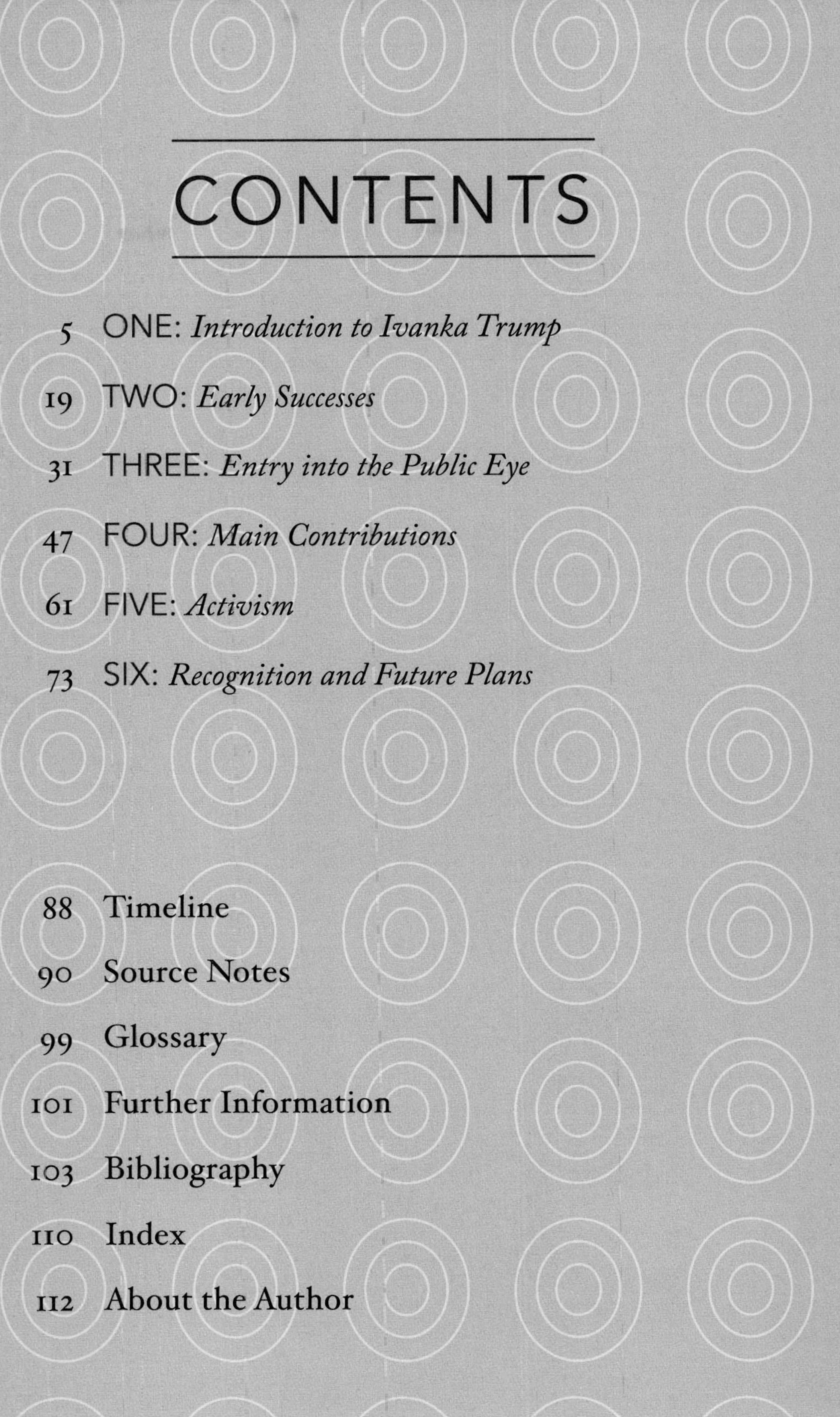

CONTENTS

REDEFINE POWER.

CHAPTER ONE

Introduction to Ivanka Trump

In business, as in life, nothing is ever handed to you. That might sound like a line coming from someone with a backstory like mine—and a load!—but if you know me and my family, you'll understand that I come by these words honestly.[1]

By the age of twenty-eight, Ivanka Trump was not only a major force in her father's widely recognized

1 Ivanka Trump, international businesswoman and role model

New York City development business, she was a published author of her first book, *The Trump Card: Playing to Work and Life.* She was born in Manhattan on October 30, 1981, the daughter of Donald Trump and Ivana Zelnickova. Her parents were among the United States' most recognizable celebrities for decades, initially as one of the glamorous power couples in the eighties, then for their highly publicized divorce, then their books written about deal making and forging one's purpose. Ivanka herself has been a public figure since she was a young girl out with her parents; as a model; as one of New York City's elite, affluent kids featured in the HBO **documentary** *Born Rich*; and more recently for her role as vice president of development and acquisitions for the Trump Organization, while also launching her own designer goods line, Ivanka Trump, and publishing two books.

Ivanka's earliest education came from watching her parents build their lives and fame in the international world of New York City. Her formal education started at the **prestigious** Chapin School in Manhattan, famous for alumni like Jackie Kennedy and Queen Noor of Jordan. As a teenager, she then transferred to the Choate Rosemary Hall boarding school in Connecticut. During her time there, a rebellious Ivanka wanted to get her navel pierced with friends, but her father called to check in on her minutes before she could go through with it—an early sign of the influence of her father in her life. After graduation, she attended Georgetown University

Always devoted to her father, Ivanka became even closer with him after her parents' divorce.

for two years before leaving and finishing cum laude with her bachelor's in economics from the Wharton School of the University of Pennsylvania, where her father had also attended. She grew up in the family business, her grandfather's real-estate and construction firm, and dreamt from the time she was a young girl of one day joining her father's business. Both of her parents developed reputations for being remarkably goal driven and energetic, raising her to see herself as responsible for upholding the family name.

The Trump Legacy

Ivanka is the fourth-generation Trump to develop business in real estate. Her great-grandfather was a German **immigrant** who made his fortune in Seattle during the Klondike gold rush as a hotel and saloon keeper who provided goods and services to miners. He later opened up a real-estate storefront in Queens, New York. Her grandfather made his fortune during New Deal **government incentives** programs to build public housing developments in Brooklyn and Queens. In order to distinguish himself from his father, Fred Jr., Donald Trump, Ivanka's father, set his sights on Manhattan during an economic slump, intent on bringing New York City back into its next period of grandeur. After two years enrolled at Fordham, he transferred to the University of Pennsylvania's business school, the Wharton School, because it had one of the few real-estate departments in the country and had been selected by his older brother. A fellow developer would say about him as a young man, "He seemed like an epic character, straight out of **Stendhal**. An ambitious boy from the provinces, full of his own ego, wanting to make his way in the city."[2]

The young Donald Trump built a reputation of being the most focused and most competitive player on the block, driven to become famous. He built the Grand Hyatt above Grand Central Terminal, Trump Tower on Fifth Avenue between Fifty-Sixth and Fifty-Seventh Streets (made famous for his purchase of Tiffany & Co.'s flagship store's **air rights** so that he could build it fifty-eight stories high), and Trump World Tower at 845 United Nations Plaza. Ivanka's bedroom growing up was on the top floor of the Trump Tower; she remembers it standing out to her that when she went to boarding school, it wasn't the Trump name that was emblazoned on the side of her dorm. In 1987, her father published *Trump: The Art of the Deal*, describing the tenets of his entrepreneurial strategies, cowritten with Tony Schwartz, a New York journalist.

In her own book *The Trump Card*, Ivanka writes that her father expected his children to not just meet, but exceed, his high expectations for them. As a result, she wanted to be more than competent, more than just good enough. She strove to be superb. Ivanka would later report that one of her first major successes was flying home after making a deal and hearing her father proclaim it to be the best he'd ever seen.

Ivanka and Her Mother

Ivanka Trump's mother, Ivana, was born and raised in Czechoslovakia. Growing up, Ivana's family was self-reliant and resourceful. They made, grew, or processed their own food. She remembers being astounded by the abundance and variety of fresh food available on the other side of the **Iron Curtain** when she first saw strawberries in February, and she realized people in other places were able to directly benefit by working harder. Even years later, as a parent, she taught her children to not waste food, to only take as much as they could eat. She described making huge turkeys for her kids so they could eat enormous turkey sandwiches and make soup. Like her daughter, she was very driven, able to see a different future for herself when she traveled to other countries to train for ski races at age twelve. Ivana's father trained her to be a competitive athlete after being born prematurely and kept in an incubator for two months. She was on the women's ski team by age fourteen. After living in Prague, Ivana moved to Montreal in the early 1970s. She could speak Czech, Russian, German, Yugoslavian, and Polish. She worked as a model and ski instructor before meeting Donald Trump. She was twenty-eight when they married, in 1977. Their daughter was born four years later.

Ivana wrote that she wanted her daughter to attend boarding school in Switzerland to gain a European flair and to learn other languages. Among her post-divorce expenses was the cost of supplying Ivanka with birthday party and hostess gifts. "I'm glad Ivanka is popular, but sometimes I wonder if anybody has a birthday party in New York City without her," she wrote.[3] Ivana credited Donald for caring about the welfare of his children, meeting over dinner to discuss them, and considering their needs in the divorce proceedings.

Ivana wrote that the *New York Post* consulted with street vendors outside their apartment for quotes to include in their **tabloid** articles about her and Donald Trump's bitter divorce in the early 1990s. *People*, *Time*, and *Newsweek* all ran the divorce story, with the *Post* publishing speculations about Ivana's upbringing and past. According to Ivana, the *Daily News* reported that the Trump divorce story boosted their circulation by thirty thousand a day, and the *Post* reported an increase of forty thousand. She wrote that the children weren't able to go anywhere—restaurants, movies, ice skating, playgrounds, walking in Central Park, or bike riding—without attracting photographers and journalists. This early experience with the media would teach Ivanka at a very young age how to go about her life on her own terms, despite what others might say publicly about her or her family.

Ivanka and her brothers continued on with life as they knew it after the divorce, with the same house, bedroom, toys, schools, vacations, and time with their grandparents. Their mother made it a point to speak well of their father to them. "If you have daughters, you want them to comport themselves with dignity no matter how hurt they are. So you have to be their role model," she would later say.[4] Both parents coordinated between their secretaries what time they should each attend school functions to avoid seeing each other. Ivanka had Catholic nannies who said prayers with her at night. "Ivanka was very brave during our family crisis—she was so dignified! The teacher told me it was incredible how she handled herself. Not only didn't her marks slide, she worked even harder and got even better grades," wrote Ivana. When Ivanka's father had a baby with his new wife Marla Maples, Ivanka told her mother, "This child didn't do anything wrong to anybody and I'm not going to be mean or nasty to her."[5] Many years later, a grownup Ivanka and her half-sister, Tiffany, would appear together on the campaign trail before reporters, united and protective of each other as sisters in the Trump family.

During spring break, Ivana took Ivanka and her brothers to their family house at **Mar-a-Lago** in Palm Beach, Florida, to escape the tabloid headlines and gossip. They spent time with her parents, swimming, playing tennis, going to the beach, and fishing. Ivanka's grandmother on her father's side often had a birthday on Mother's Day, so they would spend part of the day with their grandmother and part of the day with their mother. Ivana often entertained, hosting sit-down dinner parties for thirty-five every weekend in Mar-a-Lago, or parties in the Trump Tower, so Ivanka and her brothers grew up used to making conversation with large groups of people. Ivana would say, when her daughter was fourteen, "Ivanka is a very polished child. She knows how to greet people, how to make the small talk … You can have a wonderful conversation with her or with Eric or with Donny. They introduce themselves, start to talk, mingle with people—automatically, without thinking about it. It's their habit."[6] Ivanka also played piano for the parties her mother hosted.

Ivana believed her children should be kept busy with a wide range of activities, but she also believed that their activities should help them build skills they could use later on in life. She did not allow them to indulge casual interests unless they would also expand their practical skills for later in life. When Ivanka expressed interest in field hockey, her mother discouraged it as a boy's activity that wouldn't be as helpful to her future as another sport like karate or golf. Ivanka instead concentrated on swimming and piano. Although she took ballet for a few years, she dropped it once she grew too tall to be able to pursue a future in it. Describing her children's activities, Ivana wrote:

> *After school they have play dates, gymnastics, ballet lessons, computer lessons, piano lessons, French lessons—all kinds of different activities. They're constantly on the run, from school to karate, from karate to this or that. When they finally go to bed, they fall into a coma! But they have no time to get into trouble. Also, I feel better having them in supervised activities. In New York it's dangerous to hang around on the streets. Children have to be in some kind of planned and supervised activity, even if it's just ice-skating with a group of friends. I think it's wrong to just let them roam the streets. If you live in the suburbs or in a small town, that's something else, of course. And at the same time that they're doing all these lovely things they are trying them out to see what they might like. If you give children millions of things to do, that's how they find out what they're good at.*[7]

Ivanka and her brothers were expected to learn to both play an instrument and other languages. She accompanied her mother across the world, exploring new remote haunts such as France, China, Argentina, and Egypt. It whetted her appetite for travel, introducing her to a world of cultures where people didn't know anything about the Trump name or the lifestyle to which she was accustomed. Her mother insisted they learn to ski by age two by taking them to the top of the mountain and telling them to get to the bottom. They kept dogs, fish, birds, turtles, mice, and a duck as pets. They nursed the duck back to health after finding it outside in the street with a head wound, naming it Wobbly.

During school breaks, Ivanka and her brothers would spend a month a year in Mar-a-Lago and in the Czech Republic, Ivana's homeland, where they grew up speaking Czech with their grandmother. Ivana was a strong **disciplinarian**, and she expected her children to do errands and help around the house. Ivanka would get her the newspaper without question. Ivana wrote in 1995, when Ivanka was barely a teenager, "She does things for me as much as I do things for her … I get just as much cooperation—more, maybe—asking them nicely. 'Ivanka, would you do me a favor and go with Tony (our driver) and buy tickets for me?' She's obviously too young to go alone, but I've given her a job to do, responsibility for something, and she can be justly proud when she does it well."[8]

Ivanka's Early Dreams

Ivanka told Conan O'Brien on his late-night show a story of her earliest aspirations to build. She also wrote a slightly different version of the story in *The Trump Card*. She or her brother had received a LEGO set as a Christmas gift. She disappeared into a bedroom with it and glue, locking the door. She didn't emerge until she had designed and built a skyscraper, gluing every piece together so that it would last forever. After she got in trouble for ruining a brand new toy, her father pointed out that she'd added an extra **setback** in her structure, the recessed stair-step design at the top of very tall buildings that allows sunlight to reach the street and lower floors. She wrote that her father actually claimed the original incident as his own, that it was something he and his brother Robert had done as children with wooden blocks, and that he'd written about it in his book *The Art of the Deal*.

Ivanka grew up following her father to construction sites, observing his manner of giving orders and managing the details of completing the project. In this way, she became familiar with what it took to see a construction project through all of the details to a finished property. Ivanka was just as in awe of how her mother handled her role in developing Trump properties. "My parents are shockingly similar," Ivanka told *GQ* in a 2007 interview.[9] She recalls once traveling with her mother by helicopter to the Trump Castle Casino in Atlantic City, which Ivana was then overseeing:

I remember this so clearly. We had just gotten off the helicopter, and we were walking into the lobby, and there was this sort of—well, the whole ceiling was just this continuous chandelier, basically. I mean, thousands and thousands of lights. And she walked in, and I swear, she didn't even look up. She just points to the general manager and goes, "There's a lightbulb missing." ... I was in awe.[10]

Ivanka remembers studying the buildings outside her window from her bedroom on the top floor of the Trump Tower, noticing the different architectural details, learning their histories, noticing when they were under construction. She saw them as playthings she could reimagine, inhabited by people she knew, a world within her reach to arrange and create in. She found herself able early on to envision the future she wanted for herself, to devise the means to accomplish it in reality. As she grew up, she saw herself as someone with the opportunity to earn her own place in the world of building. Like her mother, Ivanka learned the value of women striving to fulfill their potential to the best of their ability, to set goals, to dare to turn dreams into reality. Like her father, she learned to pursue those dreams with ferocious intensity and focus.

Ivanka's Social Network

As a young girl at Mar-a-Lago, the family estate in Florida, Ivanka met Prince Charles when he came to visit when he was in town. In 2003, Ivanka was featured with nine other young, wealthy friends of Jamie Johnson, heir to the Johnson & Johnson fortune, in the HBO documentary *Born Rich*. In it, she showed her old bedroom, with posters of the bands Poison, Motley Crüe, and Bon Jovi and the television show *90210*, and the view over Central Park from the sixty-eighth floor, remarking to the camera, "Not a bad view to wake up to."[11] One of her fellow profiled wealthy children was the son of Si Newhouse, owner of Condé Nast, publisher of *Vogue*, who suggested the idea for her father's book *Trump: The Art of the Deal*.

Anna Wintour, *Vogue* editor, featured Ivanka in the magazine, with both her mother and her father's third wife, Melania, appearing on its cover over the years. Ivanka appeared in a cameo with her husband in the fourth season of *Gossip Girl* and has been featured in *Vanity Fair*, *Vogue*, *Stuff*, *Town & Country*, *Golf Digest* and many other publications. She has appeared on television shows hosted by Conan O'Orien and David Letterman. Her favorite artists include Christopher Wool and Cy Twombly, and she often posts Instagram photos in front of the artwork in her home. Her mentors include high-profile executives like Glen Senk, the former CEO of Urban Outfitters.

CHAPTER TWO

Early Successes

Ivanka Trump grew up awed by her parents, aware that they played a larger-than-life role in the world outside their family. She benefited from their attention and concern for her well-being. "As kids, all we had to do was watch them living out their dreams, filing their days with purpose and accomplishment, and know that when it was our time we could will it for ourselves," she wrote.[1] She grew up like a real-life Eloise from the children's books by Kay Thompson, roaming the hallways and crannies of the Plaza Hotel, accompanying her mother on her rounds to inspect the quality of care the carpets received when

Ivanka's early days working as a high-fashion model

vacuumed, the polish of the brass railings, the fresh flowers in the lobby, and the starch of the uniforms.

Ivanka's Early Lessons

Ivanka learned early the price of **notoriety** during her parents' divorce. Years later, she was told it was the longest-running front-page tabloid story at that time. Journalists shouted out her name as she walked to school, asking questions about her father's life with his new girlfriend. It forced her and her brothers to form a loyal alliance with each other, which would later still be apparent in their public roles with the Trump Organization and during their father's campaign for president. She also built a deeper relationship with her father once he moved out, stopping by his office every day on her way home. Emphasizing the value of these family relationships was the death of her grandfather, beloved by his grandchildren, and her childhood nanny during this time. Surviving the heartache of these losses fortified her for the challenges to come. Feeling the concentrated pain of these early losses at a young age cut through the comfort and ease of her wealthy lifestyle, something many of her peers did not experience until much later in life.

From the beginning, Ivanka's parents and grandparents made it clear that she would be expected to work for what she wanted. Her grandfather would offer her a silver dollar after the young Ivanka performed chores for her grandmother. Once she was earning her own money with modeling, she was provided a ticket for coach when she needed to travel, but she was expected to pay for the first-class upgrade if she wanted to fly first class with her mother. At any time growing up, she and her brothers were expected to help around the home when asked. When her mother hosted cocktail parties at home, she would invent reasons to be unavailable when her guests began to arrive so that Ivanka had to assume the duty of welcoming guests, learning how to behave as a poised hostess, collecting coats and taking drink orders. By fifteen, she had a summer job shadowing a **foreman** during construction of Trump World Tower. It became a point of pride to avoid asking for things from her parents that she didn't actually need or could supply herself. She did not grow up knowing she stood to inherit a generous **trust fund** when she came of age, as many of her peers did. She bought her first apartment in Trump Park Avenue with a mortgage to her father: she purchased the two-bedroom, two-bathroom apartment for $1.5 million in 2004, listing it for sale at $4.1 million after her father's winning bid for president in 2016.

Born Rich

In 2003, Ivanka appeared in Jamie Johnson's HBO documentary *Born Rich*. Although most of the other subjects attracted harsh criticisms about their snobbish attitude growing up privileged and affluent, Ivanka stood out as a gracious eighteen-year-old, appreciative for the

Born Rich cast members (*left to right*) Ivanka Trump, Si Newhouse IV, Josiah Hornblower, and Jamie Johnson

benefits she inherited. "No matter what I hear or read about my family, the fact is I'm absolutely proud to be a Trump. I'm proud of my family name and everything they've accomplished. For a while I worried that I'd always be under my parent's shadow, but I guess it's not a bad shadow to be under," she shared on screen.[2] "There was no hint of teenage rebellion on or off the screen," the film's producer, Dirk Wittenborn, told the *New York Times*. "She had a message to deliver and she delivered it."[3]

As a young teenager, Ivanka was approached by Elite Model Management. Her first magazine cover was *Seventeen* in 1997. She went on to walk the runway for Versace, Marc Bouwer, and Thierry Mugler. Modeling provided her the means to earn her own money for the fashions she wanted to wear, the opportunity to travel independent of her mother, and a chance to work in an industry uninfluenced by her father's sphere. It also provided her a testing ground for learning to interact with a diverse crowd of people outside of her parents' supervision. She learned how to present herself in her own manner. She invested most of her earnings in stocks and bonds, but a third she kept in cash so that she could buy what she wanted when the desires came up.

Because she knew she wanted to be a builder, she began to focus on a path that would aid her in that career. Law school was appealing for the skills it would develop, but an MBA seemed unnecessary as she already had experience in the field she wanted to pursue. At her father's recommendation, she sought out classes with a popular professor known for his practical application experience who became a mentor to her, Professor Peter Linneman. He suggested to her that she pursue experience with a development company other than her father's before returning to the family fold. It provided her with the opportunity to test her capability outside of the protective arm of her father and brothers. She found a position with another family firm, Forest City Enterprises, led by Bruce Ratner. Her first salary of $50,000 was significantly less than what she had made as a teenager modeling, less even than what her college peers were making in their first jobs as investment bankers.

Leaving the Nest

Trump had reached a crossroads. She was at the end of her college studies, on the verge of starting a new job in development with people she didn't already know. On the morning of her last final exam, after two hours of sleep, the phone rang, it was Anna Wintour, editor of *Vogue*, at 8:00 a.m. She was calling to offer Trump an entry-level position, an opening into the high-end world of fashion. But it wasn't a match for Ivanka's goals. Her father encouraged her to consider it. It was an opportunity for them both to measure her resolve and passion for real estate, to test whether it was actually what she wanted to do, or simply what was expected. He would later say he'd always imagined that Anna Wintour's world would ultimately claim his daughter. However, Ivanka decided to stick with the world of construction.

She joined a thirteen-person development team for a shopping center in Yonkers that did not compete with any of the Trump projects. The day before she was to start, she decided to make a trial run for the subway route she would need to take to get to work, and she got hopelessly lost. The next morning, her first day on the job, she did everything she could do to arrive prepared and ready to work in a timely manner. She found herself waiting for two hours before anyone arrived to let her in.

Describing her job performance to the *New York Times*, Bruce Ratner reported, "She did everything … from running the numbers of a deal to **negotiating** with tenants and coordinating where they would go in the center, to helping lay out the space … She was down-to-earth … She worked like everybody else. There was no special privilege about her."[4]

The job prepared Trump to handle herself in the workplace with the benign teasing that is often part of a construction site, distinguishing when it crosses over into sexual harassment and is not to be tolerated. She initially made every effort to conceal and downplay her femininity in an ultra-male work environment. Later, as she built up her confidence in the workplace, she also gained more confidence in presenting herself advantageously, expressing her personal style while also maintaining a polished, professional appearance.

Over time, she began to notice that she was advancing more rapidly than the other new hires who had joined at the same time as her. She was gaining the more interesting assignments. She also initiated requests to learn new skills, like asking an architect to show her how to use AutoCAD, a computer program for blueprints. When she was ready to return to the Trump Organization, Forest City Enterprises tried to entice her to stay with them longer, validating the experience that she'd built in her time working with them.

Joining the Family Business

At twenty-four, Ivanka joined the Trump Organization as vice president of real estate development and acquisitions. She played a leading role in development projects in New York, Chicago, Washington, DC, and as far away as Dubai. Beginning in 2005, when she joined the organization, she traveled to Panama, Colombia,

Jordan, Israel, and Kazakhstan, in addition to talking with business associates in places like Indonesia. It was the culmination of many girlhood dreams: to be building things, to be looking out over the skyline, and to be in a position to change it. At fifteen, she'd ridden in the cab of a crane up to the uppermost floor still under construction for the Trump World Tower. Once there, she spent an hour taking it all in. Now, years later, all of those heady, romantic dreams were coming to fruition.

It wasn't from a lack of effort. Even while at Forest City, she had enrolled in night classes in structural engineering and construction at New York University in order to understand the world of construction better. She continued to take classes in art history and foreign languages, finding time to fit class in around dinner meetings and late work nights. She would go on to encourage employees to share interesting newspaper articles related to Trump projects with the rest of the office. She learned to work with older, more established employees who had a different work style from her own, to become more flexible in working with their different perspectives. She became involved in updating the organization's data-management tools, integrating social media into the corporate culture, redesigning the company website, refining the company's brand and operating standards, and hiring younger employees to refresh the company.

Her father provided opportunities for her to assume leadership roles and demonstrate her developing skills. She tells the story of accompanying him to a press conference in Chicago. Under the auspices of being there to observe, after he made the opening remarks, with a wink he handed her the microphone and had her handle the talking points and answer questions. As a result, she became adept at handling pressure in front of a crowd and thinking on her feet when in the spotlight. These experiences informed her own management style in developing the talents and skills of employees she was responsible for.

Mentors and Friends

In the course of her duties, Ivanka Trump began to cultivate mentors independent of her father's circle of associates. She became friends with Rupert Murdoch, the News Corp and 21st Century Fox media mogul, and his wife at the time, Wendi Deng. Through them, she met people like Robert Thompson, then publisher of the *Wall Street Journal*, and Les Hinton, then the CEO of Dow Jones. From Murdoch, she learned the habit of stopping into the office on Sunday afternoons to check in on who was working and to get a head start on the week's activities without the distractions of scheduled meetings and calls. She also learned from painful mistakes, like thoughtlessly sending an inappropriate email to a friend who had just closed a big deal. "Who got a kickback?" she jokingly asked this usually casual CEO of a publicly traded company.[5] He immediately responded with a formal request that she retract her statement in writing. Andrew Cuomo, then the attorney general of New York (and currently the state's governor) shared with her that email is the key to prosecuting everyone in our electronic world, due to messages like the one she had sent off. Other business lessons came from Russell Simmons, the Def Jam Recordings hip-hop mogul, who shared with her that he tells his employees that stress does not equal hard work. "The mistake they make is thinking that the time they spend worrying about something is the same as actually working on it," he told her.[6]

In an appearance on *The Late Show with David Letterman*, Ivanka shared that her father was very clear about the Trump business being his and that even his children worked for him. Working for her father provided her with a foundation to learn in the trenches while adapting to a changing economy and the need to do business differently. At the same time, Ivanka launched her own businesses, while still maintaining her responsibilities to the Trump Organization. The skills she learned working in the trenches in her father's style equipped her with the ability to advance her own goals. She learned firsthand how to negotiate the deal she wanted while honoring and respecting all parties involved. This skill afforded her the opportunity to travel the world doing business, negotiating in marketplaces around the globe. It helped her build the strength and resolve to confidently negotiate for herself and her interests, for salary increases, for recognition of accomplishments, and for the ability to dress and act like a woman while working in a man's world. The Trump combination of verve, grit, and loyalty to her family name built her a reputation and brand of getting things done.

Her Relationship with Media, Branding, Public Relations, and Popular Culture

Since her parents' divorce was splashed across the front pages of tabloids when she was nine years old, Ivanka has learned to be watchful and reserved with media, while also learning how to proactively master public relations, marketing, and branding of her own endeavors. In 2012, the *Telegraph* reported that she agreed to appear on *The Apprentice* knowing she shouldn't allow too much access into her life, "It was very important for me to maintain a barrier for safety reasons and in order to give [my daughter] Arabella the option of preserving a little bit of anonymity," she said.[7]

Even this experience did not prepare her for the onslaught of public criticism during her father's campaign for president. In her comments at the 2016 *Forbes* Most Powerful Women Summit, she shared:

> The media has been vicious ... We've all had articles written about us by the business press that we say, "Hmm, you know, that wasn't exactly fair," or you know the fact-check—there's a few things off. But you know, this has been ... a different level ... I think that the bias is very, very real. And I don't think I would have said this to you even a year ago ... I think from a media perspective, it's very hard to get an accurate portrayal of who [Donald Trump] is as a person or the business he's built, his professional accomplishments. Its borderline impossible. In large parts, we've stopped even trying ...[8]

CHAPTER THREE

Entry into the Public Eye

Although familiar to many women who grew up reading fashion magazines due to her modeling, Ivanka Trump became familiar to people around the world when she joined her father and brothers on the cast of NBC's *The Apprentice* in 2006. In it, contestants competed on teams against each other to win a $250,000 single-year contract with the Trump Organization. Each episode concluded with Donald Trump dismissing the poorest-performing contestant with the words, "You're fired." The show quickly launched Ivanka into the heart of American popular culture, showcasing her high-level position in the Trump brand.

Ivanka and her father during *The Apprentice*

"I think her father really listens to her, and when I say listens to her I mean I think her father respects her a great deal, and not just because she's his daughter," said Carl Icahn, a public figure and friend of the Trumps. He added, "I don't say that lightly. I have a lot of wealthy friends who have kids and a few of them stand out, but not that many."[1] *The Apprentice* was followed by *Celebrity Apprentice*, with the *New York Times* claiming, "The best part will be watching Ivanka Trump dole out verbal punches alongside her father to tough guys."[2] Celebrity contestants have included Trace Adkins, John Rich, Carol Alt, Joan Rivers, Piers Morgan, Arsenio Hall, Bret Michaels, Cyndi Lauper, and George Takei.

In a 2006 piece about *The Apprentice*, the *New York Times* described Ivanka's relationship with her father:

> *As you'd expect from any product bearing the family name, the Trump children are carefully constructed and elegantly appointed. Perhaps more surprisingly, in an era of celebrity scions gone wild, they are also serious, self-aware and able to hold conversations in which they actually listen to what others are saying. And they ... fully understand how they can best serve the Trump Organization, and their own positions within it: by being their father's ultimate brand extensions, and getting out there and pushing his products.*[3]

Ivanka told the *Times*, "We are a different generation, and we have a different take on things than he does

... When we have that argument, he will listen to us, because he knows we represent the future."[4] Ivanka explained, according to *Forbes*, that "family businesses either work out very well or very badly, there's nothing in between ... We make a lot of effort to be respectful of one another ... As a collective we could do much more than any of us could as individuals."[5]

Stepping Up

Ivanka's appearance on *The Apprentice* cemented her reputation as a powerful woman at the helm of a global business, navigating a modern life balanced between work and family. In interviews, her father and brothers have often repeated their respect for her capabilities and her essential role in the family company. The *New York Times* closely followed her career, quizzing real-estate men about her reputation. Business associates cited the change they noticed in the family business when Ivanka stepped into a leadership role within the Trump Organization. They commented on the level of unprecedented authority she gained at the helm of her father's business. "Her father still has the final say over what to buy and how much to pay for it, but Ms. Trump now personally negotiates almost all of the company's major deals," reported the *New York Times* in 2016.[6] Even her father, notoriously critical, praised her profusely, telling the *Times*, "She is very, very trusted by me. She has great real-estate instincts and great political instincts."[7]

Soon enough, Ivanka, the original apprentice, had her own brand to distinguish in the marketplace. Ivanka Trump Fine Jewelry launched in 2007 as a luxury brand for working women, with a boutique on Madison Avenue in New York City. Especially popular in the United States, the Middle East, and Canada, it received attention in publications like *Vogue*, *Harper's Bazaar*, and *Town & Country*. Celebrities such as Oprah, Alicia Keys, Demi Moore, Blake Lively, Rhianna, and Natalie Portman have worn pieces from the collection, according to IvankaTrump.com.

Vogue magazine captured the behind-the-scenes work on Ivanka's brand management in a February 2015 profile. Johanna Murphy, then Ivanka Trump's chief marketing officer, told *Vogue*, "We are targeting millennials who aspire to have very big careers, but they are also training for marathons or learning French or starting a family. Every aspect of their life is just as important to them as their careers."[8] Ivanka added:

It's so funny seeing the way our competitors think women dress. Me and my peers, we're working really hard at being moms and sisters and professionals. There was a previous generation of women who rose through the ranks in an environment when work and life were highly compartmentalized. And I think now, because of technology, we're always on. Where there used to be work life and home life, now it's one life. And I think a lot of companies don't recognize that.[9]

Growing a Brand

In 2010, footwear and handbags were added. Outerwear became available in 2011, along with a "green" bridal collection—consisting entirely of sustainable diamonds mined in Canada with recycled gold and platinum—that was later discontinued. Ivanka said she was inspired to learn about sustainable diamond mining in her role as a founding partner of the United Nations Foundation's Girl Up campaign. By 2012, her ready-to-wear collection was released, selling at 350 department stores, including Nordstrom, Bloomingdale's, Macy's, Hudson's Bay, and Lord & Taylor, as well as independent specialty stores and on Zappos.com. Her fragrance line was released to Macy's in time for the 2012 holiday shopping season. "Where there was a void in the marketplace at our price points was a professional, hardworking, yet feminine woman," said Trump, demonstrating her refined sense of branding and marketing.[10] A collection of baby bedding sets and accessories was debuted in 2016, to be available exclusively from buybuyBaby, with a baby gift line to be released by 2018.

Love and Marriage

In 2009, Trump married Jared Kushner, a twenty-eight-year-old developer seeking to make his own mark in the New York City skyline. The grandson of Holocaust survivors, Kushner also grew up familiar with the harsh spotlight of sensationalized media after his father was

Ivanka Trump and Jared Kushner dance at their wedding reception.

imprisoned in a high-profile case for tax evasion, witness tampering, and making illegal campaign donations. As the oldest son in a large Orthodox Jewish family, Jared also demonstrated intense commitment to his family, flying to Alabama every weekend to visit his father in prison and breaking up with Ivanka for a period because she wasn't Jewish, out of respect for his grandmother's wishes. When they did marry, it was after she had converted to Judaism, taking on his family's religious practices as her own. While enrolled in undergraduate classes at Harvard, he would stay out late at night checking up on building issues with his contractor. As owner of the *New York Observer*, he earned a reputation for wanting to publish positive articles about people, avoiding the negative ones. His father shared with a reporter, "We've had a lot of experience with journalists. Some of them not so [positive]."[11]

In 2010, Trump and her husband appeared together in the fourth season of *Gossip Girl,* a wildly popular teen drama series about Upper East Side New York teenagers and their high-end lifestyle of designer clothes, champagne, parties, private schools, and personal housekeepers. The character of Lily van der Woodsen had appeared in previous seasons wearing pieces from Trump's jewelry line. Trump appeared wearing her own Naeem Khan dress. "I never miss an episode of *Gossip Girl.* I think I'm a cross between Blair Waldorf and Lily van der Woodsen when it comes to the style. I like the uptown city style and a clean-cut, streamlined silhouette," Trump told *InStyle.*[12] The episode aired on October 25, her one-year wedding anniversary.

She had met her storybook complement in Jared Kushner. A loyal and vocal defender of his father-in-law's politics, Kushner hit the attention of mainstream media for his role in winning Ivanka's father the 2016 presidential election. A few months before Election Day, James Carville, who managed Bill Clinton's 1992 campaign, spoke to the *New Yorker* about the unconventional style of the Trump campaign, saying, "Everybody that's done this for a living and got paid to do it is, like, 'Oh, my gosh, suppose this works. We're all rendered useless.' He will have destroyed an entire profession."[13] Immediately after the election, *Forbes* ran the headline, "Exclusive Interview: How Jared Kushner Won Trump the White House." *Forbes* quoted Peter Thiel, a Silicon Valley titan known for his involvement in PayPal and Facebook, as saying, "It's hard to overstate and hard to summarize Jared's role in the campaign ... If [Donald] Trump was the CEO, Jared was effectively the chief operating officer."[14] Also quoted by *Forbes*, Eric Schmidt, the former CEO of Google, stated, "Jared Kushner is the biggest surprise of the 2016 election ... Best I can tell, he actually ran the campaign and did it with essentially no resources."[15]

Multiple stories ran in the weeks during and after the 2016 presidential campaign about the power couple of Ivanka Trump and Jared Kushner, both from high-profile families in New York development, both educated at elite schools, both familiar with the pressures of life in the public eye, both loyal to family. The press drew correlations between Donald Trump, Ivanka's father, and Kushner, her husband. For example, the *New York Times* wrote:

For both men—the privileged sons of quick-tempered and domineering real estate tycoons—the legacies of their fathers loom large. More than thirty years after Mr. Trump took command of the Trump Organization and built the Grand Hyatt Hotel and Trump Tower, Mr. Kushner tapped his own family empire, Kushner Companies, to buy a Fifth Avenue skyscraper and become part owner of a giant office complex near the Brooklyn waterfront.[16]

Of the comparison between the two men, Ivanka said, "My father looked at the deals Jared was doing and saw himself in those deals."[17]

The Public Persona

Over the course of appearing publicly more frequently, both to promote her brand and her father's, Ivanka developed a cadre of superfans who described her to *GQ* during her father's presidential campaign as classy, well spoken, very brilliant, incredibly well dressed, calm mannered, and a beautiful person. During the presidential campaign, Ivanka was frequently called upon by reporters to explain her father's declarations on the campaign trail. Her memories of the media being vicious and brutal when she was a child continued to inform her experience. She described it as a whole new level that she wouldn't have felt even a year earlier. She told *Fast Company* magazine in October 2016, "I learned a long time ago that I can't control the opinions of others or what they project on me. All I can do is live my life, and I've tried to do that … The greatest comfort I have is the fact that I know my father. Most of the people who write about him don't. I do … So that gives me an ability to shrug off the things that I read about him that are wrong."[18]

Although there was some speculation that her brand would be hurt from fallout over the campaign, Pace University professor of marketing Larry Chiagouris forecasted in October 2016, just before the presidential election, that "she may come out ahead … Six months from now, whether [Donald] Trump's the president or not, I think people will hold [Ivanka] in higher regard than they would have held her six months ago."[19] A few days after the election, she received significant pushback in the media when her company advertised in a "Style Alert" that the $10,800 bracelet she was wearing in a *60 Minutes* interview was available for sale. CBS News reported, "It was not the first time Ivanka received criticism for promoting her own brand on a political stage. Less than twelve hours after introducing her father at the Republican National Convention in July, she sent a tweet about the dress she wore, a $138 garment from her own line. It sold out within a day."[20]

Campaigning for President

Over the course of the campaign, Ivanka was questioned repeatedly about her role in her father's campaign, his comments on the campaign trail about women and minorities, and whether or not she could continue her

Ivanka takes the stage to deliver her speech at the 2016 Republican National Convention in Cleveland, Ohio.

role as ambassador for both the Trump brand and her own Ivanka Trump brand, without creating conflicts of interest with her father's office as United States president. Major news sources often asked her to explain or justify her father's public statements as a presidential candidate. Repeatedly she insisted that her support came as his daughter and as an executive who had worked with him for more than a decade. Asked about support for her father among self-described white nationalists, she replied, "I categorically reject any people within a community that espouses hatred toward anyone, and my father does and has as well … I couldn't be comfortable with my father as president of this country if I thought that he could be comfortable with that type of support, and I know that he is not, that's why he's denounced it."[21]

She galvanized women voters, especially when she introduced her father at the Republican National Convention to announce his candidacy. Poised and practiced, with a ready smile, she called on the audience to support her father with her:

> *When I was a child, my father always told me, Ivanka if you're going to be thinking anyway, you might as well think big. As president, my father will take on the bold and worthy fights. He will be unafraid to set lofty goals and he will be relentless in his determination to achieve them. To people all over America, I say, when you have my father in your corner, you will never again have to worry about being let down. He will fight for you all the time, all the way, every time ... He is ready to see it all the way through, to speak to every man and every woman, of every background, in every part of this great country. To earn your trust and to earn your vote. He earned that and much more from me a long time ago. I've loved and respected him, my entire life.*[22]

Over the years, Ivanka Trump cultivated her own relationships with people who inspired her, reaching out to them with personal handwritten notes to thank them or congratulate them on news of big projects or personal accomplishments. By doing this, she afforded herself the opportunity to meet and talk with people at the top of their business. Her father described her attitude to

Vogue: "First of all, she's got tremendous heart and a great warmth, and people see that. While she can be a very tough person if she has to be, she really wants to see the best in people."[23] In *The Trump Card*, Ivanka writes about meeting with many prominent people, including Carlos Slim Helú, the Mexican billionaire who bailed out the *New York Times* with a $250 million loan, and Kayne West, the hip-hop rapper and producer. Immediately after her father's election, before he was sworn into office, those meetings included talks with well-known figures like Al Gore and Leonardo DiCaprio about climate change, as well as world leaders like Prime Minister Shinzo Abe of Japan and President Mauricio Macri of Argentina.

Once her father won the presidential election, meetings such as these came under increased scrutiny and criticism. Her friendship with Chelsea Clinton was also closely monitored and commented on throughout the campaign as Chelsea's mother, Hillary Clinton, campaigned against Ivanka's father on the Democratic ticket. "She's always aware of everyone around her and ensuring that everyone is enjoying the moment," Chelsea told *Vogue*. "It's an awareness that in some ways reminds me of my dad [President Bill Clinton], and his ability to increase the joy of the room. There's nothing skin-deep about Ivanka. And I think that's a real tribute to her because certainly anyone as gorgeous as she is could have probably gone quite far being skin-deep."[24]

Other Presidential Daughters

As daughter of a United States president, Ivanka Trump joins the ranks of such notable public characters as Martha Jefferson Randolph, Margaret Truman, Luci Johnson, Alice Roosevelt Longworth, and Julie Nixon Eisenhower, all credited with varying degrees of influence in their role as First Daughter. Alice Roosevelt Longworth, whose father, Teddy, became president after President William McKinley's assassination in 1901, may be the most famous presidential daughter for her public exploits, fashion sense, and witty barbs. She lived a long life, dying in 1980 at age ninety-six. Luci Johnson also unexpectedly found herself a president's daughter after President John F. Kennedy's assassination in 1963. She and Alice Roosevelt Longworth were also among the few daughters to have a wedding during their fathers' presidencies. Luci objected to the number of guests invited, remarking, "My parents invited only the whole nation."[25] Julie Nixon had already married the grandson of former president Dwight Eisenhower when her father took office in 1969.

Contrasting the traditional roles played by first daughters once Donald Trump was elected, the press began to speculate about Ivanka's role as a modern presidential daughter. Since his third wife, Melania, did not intend to immediately relocate to Washington, DC, rumors circulated that Ivanka would take on the role of First Lady. Due to her experience as an international businesswoman, there was talk that she would be among the president's most influential unofficial advisors.

Ivanka received much credit for humanizing her father's presidential campaign, defending or explaining his inflammatory comments and smoothing the edges of his various proclamations. Because she has also built up her own celebrity over the years, she finds herself in a unique role to bring attention to today's women's issues. Other presidents' daughters have played a part in their fathers' administrations, but never in such a public role of their own creation.

In March 2017, it was announced that Ivanka would be taking an official unpaid position in the White House. As assistant to the president, Ivanka will be able to craft a unique and unprecedented role for a First Daughter within her father's administration. Her position has her working alongside her husband, Jared Kushner, a senior advisor to the president, further consolidating and solidifying her family's influence.

CHAPTER FOUR

Main Contributions

In just a few decades, Ivanka Trump accomplished big things by making the best use of the opportunities available to her. Her role on *The Apprentice* and *Celebrity Apprentice* and their run of fourteen seasons made her famous before she and her family moved on to their next challenge in occupying the White House. Weeks after the election, it was reported that she would be one of the world's most powerful women and would occupy the offices traditionally occupied by the First Lady. Since joining her father's company, she had launched her own luxury goods lines and website, and published two books, all while

Ivanka at the helm of her own public brand

continuing in her duties with the Trump Organization. She also grew in her personal life by marrying a partner who excelled in his own pursuits in her world, holding his own in her family of ambitious real-estate men, and growing a family of three children with him.

Crafting a Life of One's Own

"They both seem to have taken the silver spoons out of their mouths and have really accomplished something," said author Michael Gross in 2009, describing Ivanka Trump and Jared Kushner, then newlyweds. Gross has written about New York's rich elite in such books as *740 Park: The Story of the World's Richest Apartment Building*. "Now we have to give them a couple of years to see if they live up to their promise."[1] According to *Crain's New York Business*, "Family, friends, colleagues and competitors almost uniformly describe Mr. Kushner and Ms. Trump … as smart, mature and hardworking. Ms. Trump is even called humble—an adjective never associated with her notoriously boastful father."[2]

The executive of a real-estate services firm who has worked with both the Trumps and the Kushners told *Crain's* that he expected the couple would "bring the real estate industry to new heights."[3] *Crain's* went on to identify the challenges that they would face as a married couple working together in the same high-risk field of a difficult real-estate market, with the added pressure of both also being from high-profile families in one of the most competitive markets in the country. However, according to Ted Clark, director of the Center for Family Business at Northeastern University, working in the same field is not without it's advantages. "They are in the same industry, so each understands what the other is going through," Clark said.[4]

By 2016, after Donald Trump won the presidential election, the *New York Times* shared that Hollywood businessman David Geffen, a longtime Democrat, was fond of the couple, despite his political differences with them. "I've known Ivanka and Jared for years," he commented. "She's a lovely, intelligent woman, and Jared has been a loyal son-in-law. [Donald] Trump depends on him. He's a very smart guy. Is he a genius? No, but guess what: The geniuses all lost."[5]

In 2011, Ivanka was back at work only days after giving birth to her first child, Arabella, similar to the tradition of other well-known, high-level women business leaders such as Sheryl Sandberg, the author of *Lean In* and chief operating officer of Facebook, and Marissa Mayer, the CEO of Yahoo! prior to its sale to Verizon. Ivanka finished brokering the deal for the 800-acre (324-hectare) Trump National Doral resort in Miami, touring the property via golf cart. Perhaps anticipating her father's bid for the White House, she took on the Old Post Office building in Washington, DC, only two blocks from the White House, to transform it into the grandest hotel in Washington. She became her father's most public ally while he ran for president, presenting the classier, calmer Trump brand amid a media firestorm of criticism. Throughout these projects, she kept a firm hand on defining her own goals while managing her brand and businesses under the Trump umbrella. "Everything has to be scalable from an economic perspective, but each venture that I get involved in also needs to reinforce, rather than undermine, the larger Trump brand," Ivanka told a reporter.[6]

A Global Brand

From 2007 to 2017, when she stepped down from her work for the Trump Organization, Ivanka Trump pursued the development of a number of properties in such locations as New York, Chicago, Las Vegas, Hawaii, Miami, Toronto, Panama, and Ireland. Three of the most recent Trump development projects, in Vancouver, Rio de Janeiro, and Washington, DC, have seen mixed success. CNN and NBC reported in late February and early March 2017 that Ivanka's brothers were greeted by protestors at the ribbon cutting for the Vancouver, British Columbia, Trump hotel. Bloomberg reported in December 2016 that the Trump brand name was removed from the beachfront Rio de Janeiro property after significant delays in construction and a criminal investigation launched in the wake of the presidential election. Meanwhile, *Town & Country* journalist Klara Glowczewska described the Washington, DC, project in their September 2016 issue, just before it was completed:

Google "Pennsylvania Avenue, Washington, DC," and you'll see image after image of a particularly photogenic section of "America's Main Street." In the foreground looms the Romanesque Revival pile of the Old Post Office Pavilion, and a short distance to the southeast floats the pale dome of the Capitol. The 1.2-mile [1.9-kilometer] stretch that begins at the White House and ends at the seat of Congress is the ceremonial heart of the nation, site of parades, processions, and protest marches. George Washington himself called it "most magnificent and convenient."[7]

In 2009, *Hotel & Motel Management* magazine reported that Ivanka told attendees at the New York Hospitality Investment Conference in New York City: "We're not going to go into a market unless we are going to be the best property in that market." She went on to explain her strategy in developing a property in the Trump tradition, describing her preference for an informal process of identifying and incorporating new talent for each new project instead of relying on in-house designers. "I really like assembling a new, fresh team for each project that we build," she shared. While relying on the Trump construction-management team to complete the basics of a new project, she emphasized her involvement from the very beginning of the planning and interview process. She also expressed a commitment to working with new people in each location because then they already have their own understanding of the market that they're working in. Using phrases like, "the least stifling and the most productive" and "we like finding outside talent that can make each project unique," she described her creative process in completing a new construction project melding both architectural and interior-design goals. "I think when you bring too many of those functions in-house, you start to repeat many of the same elements through each of your projects," she told the conference attendees. The *Hotel & Motel Management* magazine writer observed that "there are certain times when they bring successful elements from one project to other projects, but not often." Ivanka summarized, with her flair for marketing Trump properties while describing them, "Our project in Las Vegas has a very Las Vegas type of glamour and feel, our project in Chicago, while very grand, is more contemporary and modern and sleek. SoHo/New York, which will be opening this fall, while very luxurious, has a much funkier vibe to it. So, each project really fits within the context of the city and neighborhood in which it's built."[8]

The Boss's Daughter

Ivanka also, by default of doing business internationally, carved out her role and reputation in the international business world where, interestingly, reporters would describe her and her projects much more generously than those in the United States. For example, the *Sun*, a United Kingdom publication, roared with their November 11, 2016, headline: "DONALD'S TRUMP CARD: Who Is Ivanka Trump? Meet the Real First Lady and Possibly the Reason Donald Trump Won the US Election." The *Sun* went on to report that Ivanka was, as a daddy's girl, a key player in the Trump business, an icon for female voters, and soon to wield enormous influence on her father's presidency, having been the glue that held together his enterprises. The *Sun* repeated many of the highly publicized claims in mainstream media during that time. Among these was Ivanka's professional success and composure, at age thirty-five, before reporters throughout the campaign. The newspaper credited her again with helping ensure her father's election, noting the likelihood of her absorbing the role and public profile of First Lady. Being a British publication, they called her the "real power behind the throne," even crediting her with monitoring and correcting her father's behavior while campaigning.[9]

Writing for the UK journal *Business Review*, Paul Hoang gave Ivanka Trump more credit for her business accomplishments, saying:

> *Ivanka spends much of her time generating positive publicity for upcoming projects and real estate developments. She continually strives to develop the Trump brand—not surprising given that buyers are known to pay a premium of between 20–30 percent for apartments with the Trump name on it. In November 2006, all 462 units of the Trump International Hotel and Tower in Waikiki Beach, Hawaii, were pre-sold within six hours for a total of $700 million (or an average of $1.5 million per unit). In the real estate business, this is known as a "gross sellout"; the building sold out almost three full years before its completion—a world record in real estate history."*[10]

Ivanka recalled in her first book, *The Trump Card*, that she had confidence she was good but felt it didn't mean anything until she proved herself by working for someone other than her father. She felt the conflict of both high expectations because she was a Trump and the lack of any expectations at all because she was the daughter of someone who provided her with all her privileges and benefits. By working at Forest City Enterprises right out of college, she was able to gain work experience alongside her peers, out from under the arm of her father and brothers. She was able to test her hunch that she could do it, that she was capable of being something more than just the doted-upon, privileged daughter of someone else who accomplished things in the world. She was able to gain firsthand experience that she could contribute something of value to a team beyond her own immediate family. At the same time, she was able to compare her working experience to what she'd experienced watching her mother working. She saw the changes that had emerged in the years between being a young girl in the eighties and a grown, modern working woman in the twenty-first century. Reflecting on her early work experience, she wrote:

The first time I walked a construction job with my boss, I was petrified that one of the workers was going to make catcalls, and I didn't yet know how I would handle myself.

> *So I covered up—black suit, hair pulled back, that whole male-assimilation thing—to blend in a bit more. Once I finally realized that I was good at what I do, it was much easier to present myself in a way that really reflects me … You look back to the '80s, and that whole style of women in business was so extreme—the female version of the power suit, even my mom's version of suiting. There's the massive shoulder pad, the tailored silhouette. In order to garner respect, it seems that women felt they had to even out the playing field visually. These days that requirement seems to have been lifted from women in business, in America anyway.*[11]

Other Horizons

Throughout Ivanka's coming of age in the world of her father's construction and high-end development projects, she was also developing her personal style in the world of fashion. Despite turning down Anna Wintour's offer of an apprenticeship at *Vogue* right out of college, she was still contemplating business opportunities in female-oriented industries. By building on the Trump name and reputation, she was able to define new opportunities to grow her own personal brand and develop her other interests. Speaking with *Town & Country* in 2008, she traced her interest in fashion back to childhood memories of time spent with her mother:

Ivanka and her brother Donald Jr. sign their names at the topping-off ceremony for the Trump International Hotel and Tower in Chicago.

My favorite time of the day was when my mom would be getting ready for a black-tie event. She would sit at her vanity table, trying on jewelry—and the makeup in the late '80s was far different from today's in its lack of subtlety. I'd be sitting there next to her, a six-year-old trying on diamond chandelier earrings and wearing her bright-red lipstick and blue eye shadow. Just last weekend, in Palm Beach, my mom joked about it being delicious retribution that I own a jewelry store two blocks from her house in New York. She now uses my collection as her own personal wardrobe. She's in there every day raiding me out of inventory![12]

According to *Women's Wear Daily*, an industry publication, Ivanka went from being a "famous mogul's daughter to nascent fashion designer and celebrity in her own right."[13] While continuing her day job with her father's company, she launched her own website branded with her name. Her own name-branded collections of shoes, handbags, and jewelry have been sold by high-end luxury retailers like Saks Fifth Avenue and Neiman Marcus.

Ivanka's earliest times following her mother through her day helped her develop insight into the differences in taste between her mother's generation and her own. "Working with Ivanka is easy, because she knows exactly what she wants, and she's very consistent," the chief executive officer of Ivanka Trump Fine Jewelry told *Women's Wear Daily*. "She also can connect with different demographics. She has an instinct for what both younger and older women want."[14] Her perseverance, long-range game plan, and foresight served her well. By 2016, *Fast Company* reported that "net sales of the clothing arm of [Ivanka Trump's] company were up $11.8 million during the first six months of 2016 compared to the first six months of 2015."[15] The company had reportedly earned $100 million in 2015.

Speaking to a *Town & Country* reporter in October 2016, Ivanka said:

I abhor this question of "having it all." ... People talk about balance. Balance is an awful measure of things, because it implies a scale that inevitably tips. I like to look through the filter of "Is the life I'm leading consistent with my priorities?" For me, my family is the ultimate litmus test ... Do I feel I'm giving my children what they need? But I don't do everything. I wouldn't be able to do what I do professionally if I did. I don't go to the afternoon classes. I don't take my son to the sports playgroup in the middle of the day. For some people that's a compromise they aren't willing to make, and I respect that."[16]

From Women Who Work

In announcing the upcoming publication of her second book, *Women Who Work: Rewriting the Rules for Success*, Ivanka Trump posted the following statement on her website:

> Our grandmothers fought for the right to work. Our mothers fought for the choice to be in an office or stay at home. Our generation is the first to fully embrace and celebrate the fact our lives are multidimensional. Thanks to the women who came before us and paved the way, we can create the lives we want to lead—which looks different for each of us.
>
> ... I'm an executive and an entrepreneur, but I'm also—and just as importantly—a wife, mother, daughter and friend. To me, "work" encompasses my efforts to succeed in all of these areas.[17]

Remarkably, Ivanka hasn't let personal circumstances deter her from crafting a life that is her own, defined by her personal interests and aspirations. Throughout a highly visible and publicized lifestyle while growing up, division between her parents, new half siblings, and the pressure to conform to the Trump brand, she still found ways to define life by her own terms. And she didn't quit with her first early successes. She continues to search out fresh challenges and new reasons to push for something more. She also refuses to accept conventional standards of what success looks like. Instead, she keeps stepping into a public role, creating a forum to be heard, lending her voice, perspective, and experience to the conversation. Through her second book, *Women Who Work*, Trump aims to foster a broader conversation about the roles and interests of women, questioning the way our society limits women by how we structure work, family, and a sense of one's self.

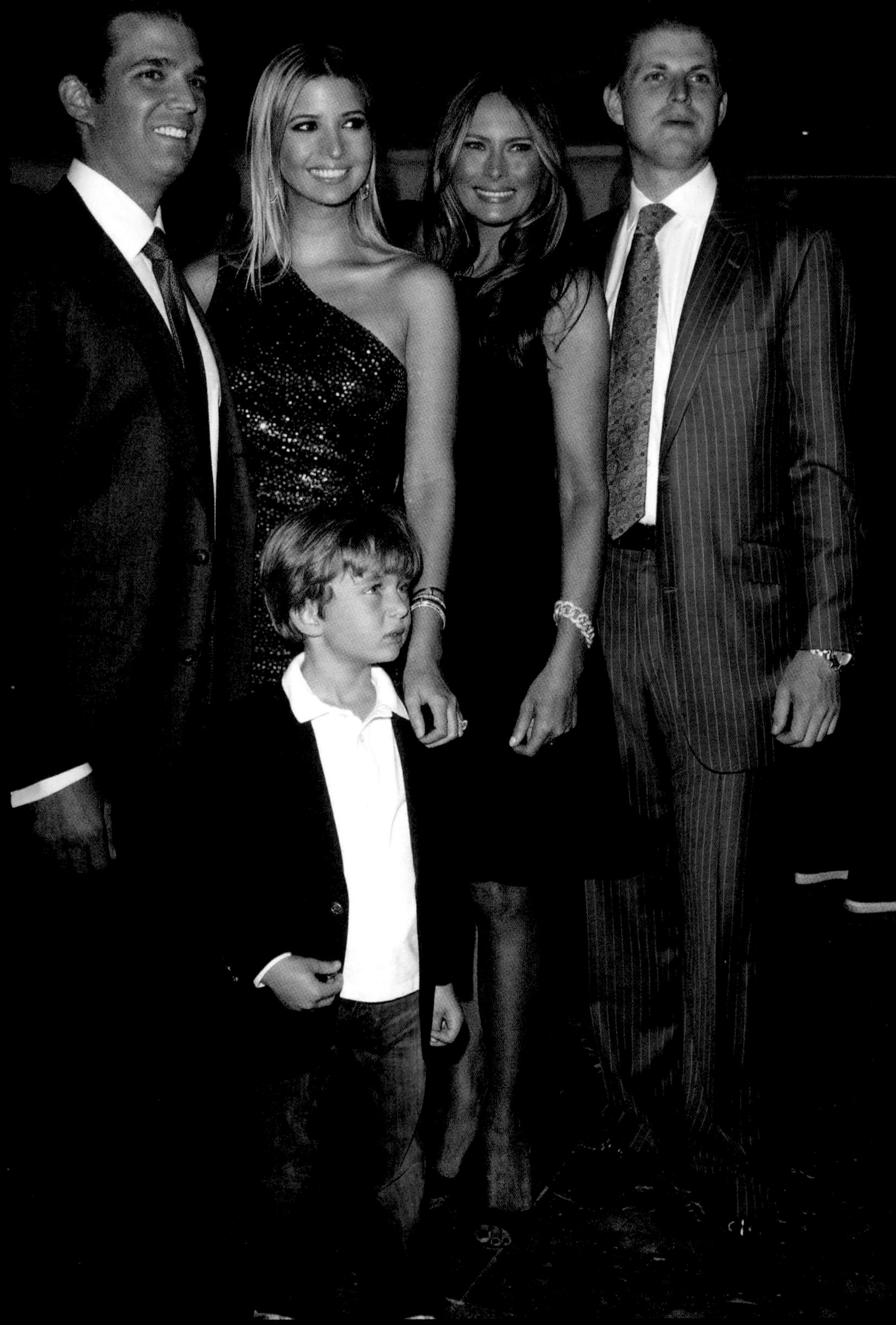

CHAPTER FIVE

Activism

Throughout her life, Ivanka Trump has been navigating what it means to be a young woman of influence in today's world. From her earliest years, she had access to the best education and opportunities available, while also seeing her own mother lead businesses and her father hire women to high-level positions in his company. At the same time, she experienced the vitriol of the tabloids toward women, their complicated relationships between each other, the men in their lives, and the competing roles they inhabit. By twenty-five, she was the youngest director on the board of a publicly traded company in the United States, thanks to her hard work but also due to her father's influence and his confidence in her abilities. Repeatedly she commented on the pressures she faced to

Trump children Donald Jr., Ivanka, Eric, and Barron pose with Melania Trump.

prove her worthiness when she already benefited from the immense privilege available to her through her father's wealth and connections. In *The Trump Card*, she shared her delight in having successfully created her own company, under her own name, "in a field so far removed from my father's sphere of influence that it feels utterly my own."[1]

Women Who Work

She added to her list of pursuits by launching #womenwhowork, the hashtag for a lifestyle concept website at ivankatrump.com that profiles the aspirations, challenges, and fears of working women. It includes posts on hosting great office parties, preparing healthy meals, and style ideas for dressing professionally. Ivanka shared in her introductory video that she hopes her daughter, Arabella, will someday find the term "working women" as odd as the term "working men." She said, "I believe that when it comes to women and work, there isn't one right answer. The only person who can create a life you'll love is you."[2]

By the time of her father's 2016 campaign, she had already established a steady stream of projects related to elevating the ambitions of girls and women. In December 2010, the United Nations Foundation announced her as a founding partner for their Girl Up campaign. In her comments about the foundation and her commitment to be involved with the campaign, Ivanka highlighted the opportunity American girls have to help girls in developing countries by sharing resources to help them develop their entrepreneurial ambitions. The Girl Up campaign's first press release urged "American girls to channel their energy and compassion to raise awareness and funds for their counterparts in the developing world."[3] Ivanka was recognized as a "champion" of the campaign, along with WNBA all-stars Alana Beard and Taj McWilliams-Franklin; TV personality and fashion photographer Nigel Barker; singer, songwriter, and American Idol finalist Crystal Bowersox; teen actress Victoria Justice; and Olympic gold medalist and swimmer Rebecca Soni. As a founding partner, Ivanka released a signature Girl Up bracelet through Ivanka Trump Fine Jewelry, with all proceeds from its sale donated to the campaign. "Girl Up's 'for girls, by girls' approach encourages American girls to become forces of global change," said Ivanka. "I am proud to be working with Girl Up and girls in this country to help ensure that all girls—no matter where they are born—get the tools they need to be educated, healthy, counted and positioned to be the next generation of leaders."[4]

Money raised through Girl Up has helped girls from places like Malawi, Ethiopia, Guatemala, and Liberia. Founding campaign partners also included Camp Fire USA, Girls Inc., MTV Networks, National Coalition of Girls' Schools, and the Women's National Basketball Association. Ivanka Trump's involvement is profiled on the Trump Organization's website; Girl Up is one of three outside causes the organization publicly supports, along with the New York City Police Foundation and the

Police Athletic League. For International Women's Day after her father entered office, Ivanka posted a video to her Instagram account showing her at the United Nation headquarters celebrating with Girl Up.

A President's Daughter

Regardless of what Ivanka proclaimed to support long before her father's presidential campaign in 2016, she would be mercilessly called to task on every aspect of her opinion and her role in supporting his campaign, particularly on the issue of whether or not he supports varied roles and freedoms for women. *Town & Country* often covered the stories relating to how Ivanka navigates her life as a Trump. She told the magazine:

> *You could also list a few comments he's made about men that are unflattering. I think he's highly gender-neutral. If he doesn't like someone he'll articulate that, and I think it's also part of what resonates about him. He'll say what he's thinking. I think that's very refreshing, because with most politicians I've witnessed, you have no idea if what's coming out of their mouths is married to their viewpoints.*[5]

Town & Country asked if she ever spoke to her father about his various declarations and insults. She answered, "Well, I'm his daughter. In a political capacity, I don't. It's his campaign. I don't feel that's my role."[6] She explained that she is foremost his daughter, and if she does challenge his behavior or comments, it is privately as his daughter, the same way any child would criticize a parent. Roger Ailes, then the chairman and CEO of Fox News, defended her credibility and authority, saying, "Ivanka is the secret weapon of the entire Trump organization. She not only has tremendous business savvy, but she's also street smart. There's no doubt she exhibits the best skills of her father, has already developed an impressive personal brand, and besides is a very nice person."[7]

"You hear that name, Ivanka, and you expect fur, leather, but she's really poised, elegant, down to earth," Mika Brzezinski, cohost of MSNBC's *Morning Joe*, told *Town & Country*.[8] Brzezinski is the daughter of President Jimmy Carter's national security adviser and knows the Trump family from her years of media work. She has often criticized Donald Trump on the air for his positions on equal pay for women, Mexican immigrants, and other issues. "You may question the views of [Donald] Trump, but when you meet his children you'll walk away questioning your own questions," she reported to *Town & Country*. "I've known enough 'daughters of'—I'm a 'daughter of.' The situation can be difficult to negotiate. I've never met one like Ivanka. She has managed to get everything good out of the situation and make it better for herself and the people around her."[9]

When pressed on the issue of her father's respect for women, Ivanka retorted to a reporter:

If he didn't feel that women were as competent as men, I would be relegated to some role subordinate to my brothers. I think this is one of his great strengths: He fully prioritizes merit and accomplishment and skill and ability over background, education, and gender ... This company, over four decades, has always had women in its highest ranks ... It's easy to look around today and say there are a lot of women in a lot of companies. It was less easy when my mother was a major executive here [as vice president of interior design] and she was surrounded by women who worked at the highest levels within this organization. I think he's one of the great advocates for women, and he has been a great example to me my whole life ... He 100 percent believes in equality of gender, so, yes, absolutely—socially, politically, and economically [he is a feminist. He has] confidence in women to do any job that a man can do, and my whole life has been proof of that.[10]

If there was any doubt about the fierceness with which Ivanka would support and promote her father's campaign for president, she stole the stage with her speech at the Republican National Convention. She praised his triumph in the lengthy, candidate-filled Republican primary, calling him a talented competitor who prevailed against the odds, as a champion of the people. She renounced any party loyalty by referring to herself as a millennial who votes according to her conscience rather than party line. She praised her father for being able to get things done as an outsider where no one else could, despite the odds, and oblivious to the critics. She talked about his commitment to his family and her treasured memories as his daughter, learning from him. She told stories of the ways in which she'd observed him over the years helping those in unfortunate circumstances, making lives better through his empathy and caring. She described his sense of justice and his commitment to being a leader of meritocracies, where incompetence is weeded out and those who deserve it are promoted, independent of background or ethnicity. She continued:

> *At my father's company, there are more female than male executives. Women are paid equally for the work that we do, and when a woman becomes a mother, she is supported, not shut out. Women represent 46 percent of the total US labor force, and 40 percent of American households have female primary breadwinners. In 2014, women made 83 cents for every dollar made by a man. Single women without children earn 94 cents for each dollar earned by a man, whereas married mothers made only 77 cents. As researchers have noted, gender is no longer the factor creating the greatest wage discrepancy in this country, motherhood is ... As a mother myself, of three young children, I know how hard it is to work while raising a family. And I also know that I'm far more fortunate than most. American families need relief. Policies that allow women with children to thrive should not be novelties, they should be the norm.*[11]

Divided Loyalties

Following her speech at the Republican National Convention, Ivanka was skewered by some political pundits. "Ivanka Trump is a talented speaker and possibly gifted politician who on Thursday night gave the best speech of this week's Republican convention. In it, she acknowledged the changing role of women in America before delivering a pack of false promises about Donald Trump's interest in addressing gender inequality," proclaimed Rebecca Traister of *New York Magazine* in outrage, with an article titled "Ivanka Is Right About Promoting Gender Equality—and Her Father Will Do the Exact Opposite."[12] Traister continued:

> *Ivanka certainly shouldn't cast a vote for her father, a man who has not only shown zero interest in addressing any of the workplace inequities his daughter laid out, but whose campaign rests partly on the premise of returning America to the earlier era Ivanka described, in which women were treated as dependents, not as economic actors or as professionals or as equals in any realm ... This is the Trump's campaign vision of women—they are wives whose economic concerns extend only to their husband's earning power ... [Donald Trump] has written that his big mistake in his first marriage, to Ivanka's mother, Ivana, "was taking her out of the role of wife and allowing her to run one of my casinos ... I will never again give a wife responsibility within my business. Ivana worked very hard ... but I soon began to realize that I was married to a businessperson rather than a wife."*[13]

Why, asked Traister, "is Ivanka trying to pass off her caveman dad as a paragon of gender equality?"[14] It was a frequently echoed plea for insight by female reporters and interviewers in multiple forums. Nevertheless, Ivanka's friends who have personal relationships with her fought back on her behalf. "She doesn't complain about anything, and she rarely expresses weakness … She elevated issues that weren't part of the Republican agenda because she cares about them," Maggie Cordish, a longtime friend of Ivanka's, told the *New York Times*.[15] Indeed, as Ivanka said in her RNC speech, and as she'd expressed to reporters in various ways over the preceding years, she doesn't see herself as locked into one narrow political ideology. Instead, she espouses the financial conservatism of her father and the Republican Party, as well as the socially progressive platform of the Democratic Party, asserting that she had voted for Hillary Clinton in previous elections.

She was criticized by reporters and bloggers across the country for her own business practices and questioned repeatedly about the inconsistencies between the policies of the Ivanka Trump line and what she espoused in interviews. For example, she was questioned about the maternity policies of one of her major branding partners. "I do control my own business practices and that's why I've chosen to offer an industry-leading eight weeks of paid leave, but obviously I can't control the practices of everyone in the universe I do business with," she told *Fast Company*.[16] *Fast Company* added that Ivanka's company does offer paid maternity leave, which puts it among only 10 percent of American businesses. Top-level Ivanka Trump employees with kids confirmed that the company is friendly to working parents. One works remotely from across the country after her family moved for her husband's job. Another employee, a single working mom, commended the company's flexible work schedule and vacation policy that make it possible for her to keep her job while parenting solo.

Ivanka told *Town & Country*:

> *One of my goals is not to preach how to live a great life. I'm not saying that if you're working at home, raising a family, that's not work. I want to disrupt the narrative around what it means to be a woman who works. The whole point of my brand is that women should be architecting the lives they want to live.*[17]

Fortune's *Most Powerful Women Summit, October 19, 2016*

Fortune's Most Powerful Women Summit gathers together female leaders in government, philanthropy, education, and the arts for wide-ranging conversations. The 2016 summit featured an interview with Ivanka Trump, where she heatedly described her respect and appreciation for her father's example in providing her with the opportunities to make her mark, as well as her love for what she does in both her father's company and her own businesses. In the interview, she discussed the challenges of dealing with the media in her role as her father's daughter during his presidential campaign, as well as what she considers to be the key policy issues that should be addressed on behalf of women and their families. She said:

> My Women Who Work initiative and my brand was launched far before the presidential cycle commenced and will continue long afterwards, and I'm incredibly proud of the work that I'm doing there, and I've always tried to maintain complete separation between that and the campaign. … I'm very proud of the business that I've built. I'm incredibly proud to play a small role in debunking this caricature of what a working woman looks like, in creating content that's actionable, that's tip-oriented for this young working woman that encourages her to architect a life that she wants to live. I've been doing it for years; I'll continue to do it. And sure, there will be critics. That's fine.[18]

CHAPTER SIX

Recognition and Future Plans

In May 2016, Ivanka posted a photo on Instagram of herself in a white dress with black lace, her red lips puckered, looking back over her shoulder beaming with the city behind her outside the window. She and her team were being recognized at the 2016 Fashion Accessories Benefit Ball in New York City with a FABB Achievement Award for her Ivanka Trump accessories line. Just a few weeks earlier, she'd been recognized by *Working Mother* in their 2016 Most Powerful Moms list. In 2012, the Wharton Business School at the University of Pennsylvania presented her with the Joseph Wharton

Ivanka arrives for her father's inauguration in Washington, DC, with her husband and their children Theodore and Arabella.

Young Leadership Award for "early success in her career and ... potential for leadership and lasting impact."[1]

Life in Washington, DC

On October 28, 2016, Ivanka Trump posted a statement to her website reflecting on the recent opening of the Trump International Hotel in Washington, DC. Completion of the hotel marked the culmination of one of her last major projects while working for the Trump Organization. She wrote:

> *This has been an unforgettable year for my family, for many reasons. We've celebrated many milestones, but one of my favorites was the grand opening ceremony for the redeveloped Old Post Office, now, Trump International Hotel, Washington, DC. A renovation is much more complex than a ground-up construction project and the redevelopment of this building was perhaps the most challenging—and gratifying—of them all. When the property was originally built in 1899, its grandeur was meant to signal to the rest of the country that Pennsylvania Avenue was America's Main Street. A full city block in the heart of Washington, DC, you didn't have to be a visionary to see its potential, despite the fact that time had taken a toll on this national treasure ... When we commenced construction, at the ground-breaking ceremony, I pledged my family's commitment to this project and to ensuring its successful execution. I told the citizens of Washington, DC, that we would not disappoint them and that we would over-deliver. I'm proud to say we've done just that.*[2]

Following the opening, there were mixed reports about how well the newest Trump Hotel in Washington was doing. As her father prepared to head to Washington, DC, and assume the presidency, Ivanka and her family were also leaving New York City for Washington, settling on a home in a heavily secured neighborhood, just blocks from the White House and from where President Obama and his family would be renting a home. Now that the Trumps are in Washington, alongside their internationally established family brand, it seems likely that they will do what they've always done: focus on getting the job done their own way, navigating the risks and failures while ignoring the critics. The typical Washington, DC, hotel cost is reported to average about $300 per night, while the brand new Trump hotel runs between $700 and $1,000 per night, significantly more. Ivanka explained her family's business strategy to Lloyd Grove, a journalist for *Entrepreneur*, in 2008: "Obviously you look for growth and you look for basic stability. You also have to look at the price point that you can sell for, even if you're selling for a premium of 50 percent to market, which is not unusual, especially when we enter emerging markets. In Panama, we sold at a 500 percent premium to anything the luxury market has ever experienced prior to our entry. Even in Hawaii, a year and a half ago, we sold $729 million worth of real estate in six hours—10 percent hard deposit for a 50 percent premium to luxury market. Very sizable premiums relative to the high-end luxury competition in those markets."[3] In a place like

Washington, DC, an international meeting place between national and world leaders, it seems likely that the Trumps will again shake things up for their competitors, changing the game for everyone else while they play it their own way.

Family Life

In an unusually intimate interview with *People* magazine, Trump shared what her family life has been like since the arrival of her third child, Theodore James, in March 2016, adding to the responsibilities of parenting daughter Arabella, born in 2011, and Joseph, born in 2013. "My life is chaotic right now. I'm exhausted 90 percent of the time … Being a mother is the most rewarding experience, but also the most wild and stressful."[4] She praised her husband for his active role in parenting, describing their developing routine as parents of three very young children. She explained that they work hard during the week, relying on a nanny for daily childcare support, while keeping their weekends open to disconnect from phones and emails, in order to reconnect with each other and their children. She also acknowledged her reliance on the other women in her family, including her mother-in-law, for support and back-up with taking care of her children. In particular, she cited the example of her sister-in-law Vanessa, who has five children with Ivanka's bother Donald Jr. Ivanka said she was awed by the fluidity with which Vanessa could handle the large brood of cousins—both Ivanka's children and her own.

Ivanka is still clearly figuring out how to balance the needs of each of her three children amid her weekly duties, echoing her mother's reminiscences about the idiosyncrasies of raising her very different children. "I think everyone has to work extra hard to make the older siblings feel loved and secure of their place when you're going through a time of transition. I try to carve out special time with each of them. Joseph loves playing with cars. Arabella could read with me for hours. Poor Theo. He's always the one where they're interrupting his time with me. But ultimately I think it will be good for him," she shared with *People*.[5]

It has been of concern how the Trump family will navigate conflicts of interest between their business and political office. Initially there was speculation that Donald Trump would leave his company to his children to manage, and indeed, that is what he chose to do, placing his two oldest sons in charge of the Trump Organization. However, this still leaves open concerns about conflicts between his relationships with foreign nations and his family's business interests with those nations. Ivanka has also stepped down from her role with the Trump Organization, in addition to appointing a president to run her own company. Because the Trump family has business interests in nations across the globe, in places like India, Indonesia, and Turkey, lawyers have declared that the only way of fully resolving four years of constant ethical dilemmas would be to liquidate all assets and have them placed into a blind trust. This would mean that the wealthiest president in United States history would have no knowledge of how his immense wealth is managed while he is in office. Even payments to the Trump International Hotel in Washington from diplomats hosting events or staying as guests are problematic if Donald Trump benefits while in office as president.

Ivanka and her father continue to both enchant and incense the American public and media, evoking the rage and frustration that Americans feel in today's changing global market, as well as Americans' relentless optimism that the next generation can do it better by doing it differently. These traits seem to complement each other as father and daughter move forward to the next era of their family brand and personal ambitions. Ivanka seems to do her best work in acting as a counterbalance to her father's tempestuous and inflammatory manner of doing business. "Where Donald Trump was brusque, Ms. Trump was tactful. Where Mr. Trump came off self-centered and easily distracted, she was self-effacing and sharply focused, traits she displayed from her earliest days growing up on the Upper East Side," reported the *New York Times*.[6] Together, they continue to be formidable.

As Ivanka, her father, and their family continue to plot an ambitious course between the president's office, international business, and global influence, they will continue to encounter criticism from opposing camps, while they also continue to electrify their support base with fresh confidence and enthusiastic support. The *New York Times* noted that while Prime Minister Shinzo Abe of Japan met with Ivanka and Donald Trump, then the president-elect, in New York City, at the same time, in Tokyo, "another exclusive gathering was already underway: a two-day private viewing of Ivanka Trump products, teeming with Trump-branded treasures like a sample of the pale pink dress Ms. Trump wore to introduce her father at the Republican National Convention." Furthermore, according to the *New York Times*, after two years of deal making and discussions, Ivanka was "nearing a licensing deal with the Japanese apparel giant Sanei International ... The largest shareholder of Sanei's parent company is the Development Bank of Japan, which is wholly owned by the Japanese government." Over that period of time, Ivanka had succeeded in fascinating the Japanese with her personal celebrity and charisma. According to a magazine editor present at the Tokyo viewing, "At the moment, Ivanka is even more popular here [in Japan] than Mr. Trump."[7] Perhaps because the deal with Sanei could have been seen as a major conflict of interest, Ivanka backed away from it shortly before her father's inauguration.

Both the New Yorker and the New York Times report that Ivanka is considered more popular than her father in China as well. The Chinese credit her for being rich, beautiful, and smarter than her father, while also modeling Confucian values of family loyalty. Young women in China look up to her as a model of modern femininity, with her own beautiful family. They are inspired by her success as a businesswoman in her own right, outside of her family's dynasty. While many in China praise her as elegant, hardworking, and ambitious, others criticize her for trying too hard, and for still being dependent on and protected by her father's power.

She is known as Yi Wan Ka and is compared to Xi Shi, China's legendary most beautiful woman, who captivated and humbled kings with her beauty and charm. Early in his presidency, Donald Trump suggested that the United States would begin to more directly challenge China by recognizing Taiwan as independent of Chinese authority. Shortly after, apparently to smooth over tensions between the two countries, Ivanka visited the Chinese embassy in Washington, DC, with her family for Lunar New Year celebrations. Prime-time Chinese news covered the visit. Two days before, Ivanka had Instagrammed a photo of her youngest child, Theodore, playing with wooden blocks painted with Chinese symbols. In April 2017, her five-year-old daughter, Arabella, who started learning Chinese from her Chinese nanny when she was eighteen months old, serenaded Chinese president Xi Jinping and his wife with a Chinese song during their visit to Mar-a-Lago.

Building a Network

Every day that led up to the transition to a new president and administration brought out new stories speculating about the Trumps' next steps. *Politico* magazine, which reports news about Congress, the White House, campaigns, lobbyists and issues, confidently reported in early January 2017, "As Ivanka Trump seeks to define the unique and powerful role she is expected to play in her father's orbit, she has been leaning over the past month on Goldman Sachs partner Dina Powell, president of the Goldman Sachs Foundation, as a top adviser on policy and staffing."[8] Included in the report was praise from a former George W. Bush administration official for Powell's ability to execute big ideas, as evidenced by her critical work during Bush's presidency in empowering women in the Middle East. The same official also commended Ivanka for her intelligence in seeking out such credible expertise. Describing Powell, *Politco* wrote:

> *At Goldman Sachs, Powell, forty-two, is viewed as a leading voice on women's empowerment in the workplace, overseeing "10,000 Women," one of the investment bank's biggest charitable initiatives, which focuses on helping female entrepreneurs around the world. Powell, an Egyptian-born, Dallas-raised, fluent Arabic speaker, also served as chief of the personnel office in the White House under President George W. Bush, and as an assistant secretary of state for educational and cultural affairs in the Bush administration. Powell, multiple sources said, has become an invaluable resource to Ivanka Trump, who wants to position herself as a national leader on women's economic empowerment. In Powell, she has also found an adviser who knows her way around the White House, and who knows about staffing, which Ivanka Trump will also need help with if she fills the expected role of functional first lady.*[9]

Soon after Donald Trump's inauguration, Powell was named a senior economic advisor to the president. In March 2017, she was given a spot on the National Security Council, as a deputy national security advisor for strategy.

Politico continued in their evaluation of Ivanka's capacity to balance her support for her father's administration with her iconic status for women expecting progress on key issues of concern to them, especially for mothers employed in the traditionally male corporate hierarchy. Along with other news outlets, *Politico* was dismissive and skeptical that Ivanka, in her relative inexperience in policy matters, could have any meaningful influence on top issues. For example, after she commented on climate change and held a widely publicized meeting with former vice president Al Gore, a climate change denier was nonetheless named head of the Environmental Protection Agency. Alliances with rock-solid female leaders like Powell stand to go far in helping Ivanka achieve her ambitions for a lasting policy influence on women's issues. These friendships and partnerships also stand to serve her as sources of support while she learns to navigate a new work environment populated by a different demographic of players and interests. For now, all that we know about Ivanka's plans is who she's been so far and what she's shared about where she hopes to go. Celebrity fashion editor Andre Leon Talley pointed out in *Vogue's* "Movers and Shakers" feature that:

> *She could have turned out to be a postdeb dilettante, a modern-day Etti Plesch, Countess Esterhazy, who ended up marrying six times. She could have been on the slopes of Aspen or Cortina d'Ampezzo or a red-carpet regular. But she's grounded, often flies JetBlue, and totes her own carry-ons when traveling. "I stopped carrying luxury-logo luggage when my brother was not as chivalrous about carrying it for me. He said, 'If you're going to bring that thing, which weighs 40 pounds [18 kilograms] empty, you're carrying it," [Ivanka said].*[10]

Regardless of who it is, almost without exception, people who comment on what they know of Ivanka through personal experience mention her grace and presence, her ability to acknowledge the privilege she's inherited while also discretely finding ways to demonstrate her own earned prowess, her personally developed sensitivity to the travails of others, and her own vision for her future. From her youngest days in front of a camera during her parents' public divorce and the controversy that has simmered around her family in the decades since, she has maintained her own quiet insistence on a life of her own creation.

Looking to the Future

When asked several years ago what she sees in her future, she responded:

> *I think I'll be exactly where I am today, in ten years, in twenty years, with a lot more experience under my belt. One of the great things about what I'm doing is it's a really unique experience from an educational perspective, to A, be able to work so directly with somebody with the experience of my father, B, be able to have jobs that are ongoing and in various stages of construction across so many different cultures, in so many areas of the world, utilizing so many different architects and interior designers and working with them, learning from them. Each job is so unique and so specific that I get to learn an enormous amount in a much shorter period of time.*[11]

These days, the current news attention to Ivanka and her family centers on their new life in Washington, DC. Ivanka Trump the company is now held in a trust for as long as her father is president, and she has almost no input into how the company is run. Abigail Klem, a registered Democrat, former lawyer, and longtime company employee is now company president. She speaks proudly of her respect for Ivanka and her desire to lead the company with integrity. There have been reports that the brand may have suffered from post-election protests, with large retailers like Nordstrom and Neiman Marcus dropping the brand. Other reports, including from Klem, suggest instead that brand popularity has actually increased significantly since the beginning of the Trump presidency, due to increased exposure and political support, despite it being barred from using Ivanka's image to promote the brand. One report claims that the brand rose in sales rankings from number 550 to number 11 between January and February 2017.

In mid-March 2017, *Politico* reported that Ivanka was stepping into an official role in the White House by occupying an office on the second floor in the West Wing, next to senior advisor Dina Powell. She would be granted a security clearance and receive a government-issued communication device. This indicated that Ivanka would act as a full-time staffer in her father's administration, though without an official position or salary. As evidence of her growing role, she was seated beside German chancellor Angela Merkel for the chancellor's first visit with the Trumps in the White House.

Because Ivanka was the daughter of the president, not an official employee of the administration, it was unclear how she would be held accountable to ethics rules for conflicts of interest, though she stated her intention to voluntarily comply with the same rules she would be held to as a federal employee. While this arrangement raised eyebrows, it was consistent with the role she has always played in working with her father, acting as his right hand, gathering information, and providing perspective for him. Norm Eisen, formerly an ambassador to the Czech Republic and known as the ethics czar in Barack Obama's administration, observed to *Politico*, "They're not saying she's going to voluntarily subject herself to ethics rules to be nice … There's recognition that they're in very uncertain territory here. The better thing to do would be to concede she is subject to the rules. It would create some outside accountability, because if she can voluntarily subject herself to the rules, she can voluntarily un-subject herself to the rules … You might be inclined to view this differently and more generously if the White House had shown a stronger commitment to ethics enforcement."[12]

In late March 2017, it was announced that Ivanka would instead be appointed to an official position in her father's administration, though she would still not receive a salary. She was given the title "assistant to the president." Her move from unofficial advisor to official government employee was intended, at least in part, as an answer to the lingering ethics concerns expressed by people like Eisen. In her new role, Ivanka's compliance with ethics rules is mandatory, not voluntary. In a statement about the change, Ivanka said, "I have heard the concerns some have with my advising the president in my personal capacity while voluntarily complying with all ethics rules, and I will instead serve as an unpaid employee in the White House Office, subject to all of the same rules as other federal employees."[13]

Things appear to have quieted down for Ivanka's home life. In the weeks following her family's appearance at the presidential inauguration ceremony in late January, there were her usual Instagram posts sharing moments with her family. A popular post showed her youngest child, Theo, crawling for the first time at the White House. Other posts included images of her children on the swings at a park in Washington, DC, and making treats at home to celebrate Jewish holidays. Other stories commented on the history of their new home, on Ivanka and her husband out jogging together, and on Arabella's new school. Throughout the continued controversy surrounding her father's every move and decision, she continues on as she always has, loyal to family and quietly enjoying the pleasures of the newest chapter in her life, among those she loves best, in her own way and on her own terms.

Exceptional Daughters

Doug Wead, author of *All the Presidents' Children*: Triumph and Tragedy in the Lives of America's First Families, was inspired to write his book after researching and writing a forty-four-page report on the lives of presidential children for President George H. W. Bush in 1988. In the book, Wead observes that while many presidential children have led troubled lives, presidential daughters have often been exceptions. Wead writes:

> Research showed that being related to a president brought more problems than opportunities. There seemed to be higher than average rates of divorce and alcoholism and even premature death … The expectations set by the public for presidential children—and by the presidential children themselves—were murderously high … On the bright side, one encountered an expansive oasis in this bleak landscape … [Presidential daughter] Helen Taft Manning became dean of Bryn Mawr College when she was only twenty-five years old, and fought tirelessly for the rights of working women … The daughters of Woodrow Wilson battled for woman suffrage and for safer working conditions for female factory workers … There is no record of presidential daughters committing suicide or destroying their lives with alcohol, or wasting time on get-rich-quick schemes, or thinking that the world owed them a living, as in the case of too many presidential sons. Perhaps it is a reflection of the unique feminine nature, an ability to internalize and adapt rather than to combat the circumstances and command the environment.[14]

Timeline

1981
Ivanka Trump is born in Manhattan, New York.

1997
Appears on the cover of *Seventeen.*

2004
Graduates summa cum laude from the Wharton School at the University of Pennsylvania.

2005
Joins the Trump Organization.

2006
Joins the cast of *The Apprentice*.

2007
Launches Ivanka Trump Fine Jewelry, followed by the Ivanka Trump Lifestyle Collection.

2009

Publishes her first book, *The Trump Card: Playing to Win in Work and Life*; converts to Judaism; marries real-estate developer and businessman Jared Kushner.

2011

First child, Arabella, is born.

2013

Second child, Joseph, is born.

2014

Launches www.IvankaTrump.com for "Women Who Work"; breaks ground for the Trump International Hotel in Washington, DC.

2016

Joins her father on the campaign trail for United States president; her third child, Theodore, is born.

2017

Moves her family from New York City to Washington, DC; publishes her second book, *Women Who Work: Rewriting the Rules for Success*.

3. Dave Itzkoff, "Reluctant Apprentices" *New York Times*, December 31, 2006, http://www.nytimes.com/2006/12/31/arts/television/31itzk.html.

4. Ibid.

5. Natalie Robehmed, "Ivanka Trump on Being the Other Trump," *Forbes*, May 12, 2016, http://www.forbes.com/sites/natalierobehmed/2016/05/12/being-the-other-trump-ivanka-trumps-mission-for-success-despite-her-dad/#4db832ae6ff6.

6. Mahler, "In Campaign and Company, Ivanka Trump Has a Central Role."

7. Ibid.

8. Jonathan Van Meter, "Ivanka Trump Knows What It Means to Be a Modern Millennial," *Vogue*, February 25, 2015, http://www.vogue.com/11739787/ivanka-trump-collection-the-apprentice-family.

9. Ibid.

10. David Moin, "Ivanka Trump Plays Another Card," *Women's Wear Daily*, March 28, 2012, http://go.galegroup.com/ps/i.do?p=ITOF&sw=w&u=nysl_we_becpl&v=2.1&it=r&id=GALE%7CA285340980&asid=65a9f27fe1d9efce11a3dd2212e4b53e.

11. Jeremy W. Peters, "Citizen Kushner," *New York Times*, June 24, 2011, http://www.nytimes.com/2011/06/26/fashion/life-in-the-fishbowl-for-jared-kushner.html.

12. Kendall Herbst, "Ivanka Trump Talks Gossip Girl Cameo," *InStyle*, October 27, 2010, http://www.instyle.com/news/ivanka-trump-talks-gossip-girl-cameo.

13. Lizzie Widdicombe, "Ivanka and Jared's Power Play," *New Yorker*, August 22, 2016, http://www.newyorker.com/

magazine/2016/08/22/ivanka-trump-and-jared-kushners-power-play.

14. Steven Bertoni, "Exclusive Interview: How Jared Kushner Won Trump the White House," *Forbes*, December 20, 2016, http://www.forbes.com/sites/stevenbertoni/2016/11/22/exclusive-interview-how-jared-kushner-won-trump-the-white-house/#106f5fa22f50.

15. Ibid.

16. Michael Barbaro and Jonathan Mahler, "Quiet Fixer in Donald Trump's Campaign: His Son-in-Law, Jared Kushner," *New York Times*, July 4, 2016, https://www.nytimes.com/2016/07/05/us/politics/jared-kushner-donald-trump.html.

17. Ibid.

18. Anjali Mullany, "Ivanka Trump Doesn't Flinch," *Fast Company*, October 17, 2016, https://www.fastcompany.com/3063963/behind-the-brand/ivanka-trump-doest-flinch.

19. Ibid.

20. Caroline Linton, "Ivanka Trump Takes Fire for Hawking $10,800 Bracelet Worn on '60 Minutes,'" CBS News, November 15, 2016, http://www.cbsnews.com/news/ivanka-trump-label-promotes-bracelet-after-60-minutes-interview.

21. Mullany, "Ivanka Trump Doesn't Flinch."

22. Ivanka Trump, "2016 Republican National Convention Speech," Delivered July 21, 2016, Cleveland, OH, Posted on YouTube July 21, 2016, https://www.youtube.com/watch?v=0JdxeWyL8VU.

23. Van Meter, "Ivanka Trump Knows What It Means to Be a Modern Millennial."

24. Ibid.

25. Doug Wead, *All the Presidents' Children: Triumph and Tragedy in the Lives of America's First Families* (New York: Atria Books, 2003).

Chapter 4

1. Theresa Agovino, "Javanka! Real Estate's Newlyweds," *Crain's New York Business*, November 15, 2009, http://www.crainsnewyork.com/article/20091115/FREE/311159973/javanka-real-estates-newlyweds.

2. Ibid.

3. Ibid.

4. Ibid.

5. Alessandra Stanley and Jacob Bernstein, "Will Ivanka Trump Be the Most Powerful First Daughter in History?" *New York Times*, December 3, 2016, http://www.nytimes.com/2016/12/03/fashion/ivanka-trump-first-daughter.html?.

6. Sophia Chabbott, "Ivanka Trump Sets Aggressive Goals, Naturally," *Women's Wear Daily*, February 1, 2010, http://go.galegroup.com/ps/i.do?p=ITOF&sw=w&u=nysl_we_becpl&v=2.1&it=r&id=GALE%7CA221753198&asid=8ed97dd5e572d00aa0c245d088e7c9bd.

7. Klara Glowczewska, "I Took a Behind-the-Scenes Tour of the New Trump Hotel in Washington DC," *Town & Country*, September 9, 2016, http://www.townandcountrymag.com/leisure/travel-guide/news/a7784/trump-hotel-washington-dc-opening.

8. Paul J. Heney, "Ivanka Trump Keeps Hotels Contextual," *Hotel & Motel Management*, October 5, 2009, http://go.galegroup.com/ps/i.do?p=ITOF&sw=w&u=nysl_we_becpl&v=2.1&it=r&id=GALE%7CA212412711&asid=ddf51d0536f5fdbe97964f510acd19bd.

9. Caroline Iggulden, "Donald's Trump Card: Who Is Ivanka Trump? Meet the Real First Lady and Possibly the Reason Donald Trump Won the US Election," *Sun*, November 11, 2016, https://www.thesun.co.uk/news/2161436/ivanka-trump-first-lady-donald-us-election-2016.

10. Paul Hoang, "Ivanka Trump: Paul Hoang Profiles the Highly Successful American Businesswoman, Fashion Model and Heiress," *Business Review*, November 2010, http://go.galegroup.com/psi.dop=ITOF&sw=w&u=nysl_we_becpl&v=2.1&it=r&id=GALE%7CA241529534&asid=391470048b61e9176fa29817cb915890.

11. Ivanka Trump, *The Trump Card.*

12. Kristina Stewart Ward, "Daddy's Little Girl: She May Be Donald's Daughter, but Make No Mistake: Ivanka Trump Is Her Own Woman," *Town & Country*, July 2008, http://go.galegroup.com/ps/i.do?p=ITOF&sw=w&u=nysl_we_becpl&v=2.1&it=r&id=GALE%7CA182524809&asid=4e93fb90d1acdf5b7637cb11cb9ada08.

13. Sarah Haight, "Ivanka Trump, Mogul: Fashion Line Grows, but Is She For Real?" *Women's Wear Daily*, August 3, 2010, http://go.galegroup.com/ps/i.do?p=ITOF&sw=w&u=nysl_we_becpl&v=2.1&it=r&id=GALE%7CA234162854&asid=36e73a244a972e68d74e99d3344b1359.

14. Ibid.

15. Mullany, "Ivanka Trump Doesn't Flinch."

16. Tim Teeman, "Ivanka Trump Talks Being a Mogul, a Mother, and More," *Town & Country*, October 19, 2016, http://www.townandcountrymag.com/society/money-and-power/a4616/ivanka-trump-2016.

17. Ivanka Trump, "Women Who Work," Accessed January 3, 2017, http://ivankatrump.com/book.

Chapter 5

1. Ivanka Trump, *The Trump Card.*
2. Ivanka Trump, "Women Who Work."
3. "United Nations Foundation Launches Girl Up," United Nations Foundation, September 30, 2010, http://www.unfoundation.org/news-and-media/press-releases/2010/united-nations-foundation-launches-girl-up.html.
4. Ibid.
5. Teeman, "Ivanka Trump Talks Being a Mogul, a Mother, and More."
6. Ibid.
7. Ibid.
8. Ibid.
9. Ibid.
10. Ibid.
11. Ivanka Trump, "2016 Republican National Convention Speech."
12. Rebecca Traister, "Ivanka Is Right About Promoting Gender Equality—and Her Father Will Do the Exact Opposite," *New York Magazine*, July 22, 2016, http://nymag.com/thecut/2016/07/ivanka-trump-rnc-speech-wrong.html.
13. Ibid.
14. Ibid.
15. Stanley and Bernstein, "Will Ivanka Trump Be the Most Powerful First Daughter in History?"
16. Mullany, "Ivanka Trump Doesn't Flinch."

17. Teeman, "Ivanka Trump Talks Being a Mogul, a Mother, and More."

18. White, Reilly, and Chan, "Read Ivanka Trump's Remarks at the Fortune Most Powerful Women Summit."

Chapter 6

1. Jane Reed, "Donald Trump's Daughter, Ivanka, Went to Georgetown and University of Pennsylvania," *University Herald*, October 8, 2016, http://www.universityherald.com/articles/43296/20161008/donald-trump-daughter-ivanka-went-georgetown-university-pennsylvania.htm.

2. Ivanka Trump, "From Ivanka's Desk: A Grand Opening," IvankaTrump.com, October 28, 2016, https://ivankatrump.com/ivankas-desk-grand-opening.

3. Lloyd Grove, "Ivanka Trump," *Entrepreneur*, November 10, 2008, https://www.entrepreneur.com/article/198386.

4. Charlotte Triggs, "Inside Ivanka Trump's Chaotic Life Raising Three Children with Husband Jared Kushner: 'I'm Exhausted 90 Percent of the Time,'" *People*, July 21, 2016, http://celebritybabies.people.com/2016/07/21/ivanka-trump-raising-three-children-jared-kushner-exhausted.

5. Ibid.

6. Stanley and Bernstein, "Will Ivanka Trump Be the Most Powerful First Daughter in History?"

7. Matt Flegenheimer, Rachel Abrams, Barry Meier, and Hiroko Tabuchi, "Business Since Birth: Trump's Children and the Tangle That Awaits," *New York Times*, December 4, 2016, http://www.nytimes.com/2016/12/04/us/politics/trump-family-ivanka-donald-jr.html?_r=0.

8. Annie Karni, "Ivanka Trump Turns to Goldman Sachs Partner for Advice," *Politico*, January 5, 2017, http://www.politico.com/story/2017/01/ivanka-trump-goldman-sachs-233234.

9. Ibid.

10. "Movers and Shakers," *Vogue*, January 2008, http://go.galegroup.com/ps/i.do?p=ITOF&sw=w&u=nysl_we_becpl&v=2.1&it=r&id=GALE%7CA177657587&asid=e136948a6736b2153fa8197f947763d2.

11. Grove, "Ivanka Trump."

12. Annie Karni, "Ivanka Trump Set to Get West Wing Office as Role Expands," *Politico*, March 20, 2017, http://www.politico.com/story/2017/03/ivanka-trump-white-house-236273.

13. Maggie Haberman and Rachel Abrams, "Ivanka Trump, Shifting Plans, Will Become a Federal Employee," *New York Times*, March 29, 2017.

14. Wead, *All the President's Children*.

GLOSSARY

air rights The property interest in the "space" above Earth's surface. Generally speaking, owning, or renting, land or a building includes the right to use and develop the space above the land without interference by others.

disciplinarian A person who believes in or practices firm discipline.

documentary A movie or a television or radio program that provides a factual record or report.

foreman A worker, especially a man, who supervises and directs other workers.

government incentives Governments structure economic incentives to encourage certain behavior—for example, taxing investment income lower than earned income to encourage investment and saving.

immigrant A person who comes to live permanently in a foreign country.

Iron Curtain The border separating the former Soviet bloc and the West prior to the decline of communism that followed the political events in Eastern Europe in 1989.

Mar-a-Lago A landmark estate that has a history of attracting wealthy socialites and ambassadors from across the world.

negotiating To try to reach an agreement or compromise by discussion with others.

notoriety The state of being famous or well known for some bad quality or deed.

prestigious Inspiring respect and admiration; having high status.

setback A steplike recession in a wall or any of a series of such recessions in the rise of a tall building.

Stendhal The pen name for Marie-Henri Beyle, a nineteenth-century French writer highly regarded for the acute analysis of his characters' psychology. Considered one of the earliest and foremost practitioners of realism.

tabloid A style of journalism that emphasizes sensational crime stories, gossip columns about celebrities and sports stars, and astrology.

trust fund A fund comprised of a variety of assets intended to provide benefits to an individual or organization. A grantor establishes a trust fund to provide financial security to an individual, most often a child or grandchild, or an organization, such as a charity or other nonprofit organization.

FURTHER INFORMATION

Books

Bausum, Ann. *With Courage and Cloth: Winning the Fight for a Woman's Right to Vote.* Washington, DC: National Geographic Children's Books, 2004.

Newton-Small, Jay. *Broad Influence: How Women Are Changing the Way America Works*. New York: Time Home Entertainment, Inc., 2016.

Trump, Ivanka. *Women Who Work: Rewriting the Rules for Success.* New York: Penguin, 2017.

Websites

Girl Up: Uniting Girls to Change the World
https://girlup.org

Learn more about the United Nations Foundation's campaign to empower girls from around the world.

Lean In: Women, Work, and the Will to Lead
https://www.leanin.org

Lean In is a nonprofit organization and online community dedicated to helping all women achieve their ambitions, changing the conversation from what we can't do to what we can do.

The Trump Organization
http://www.trump.com

The official website of the Trump family's business organization. Includes portfolio (real estate, hotels, golf, entertainment, and television), publications, and merchandise.

The White House
https://www.whitehouse.gov

See the president's daily schedule, explore behind-the-scenes photos from inside the White House, and find out all the ways you can engage with the highest office of the United States.

Women in Business TED Talks
https://www.ted.com/topics/women+in+business

View a collection of speeches about women in business from TED, an organization committed to sharing exciting and innovative ideas with the world.

Video

Ivanka Trump at Skift Global Forum 2015, "Defining the Future of Travel"
https://www.youtube.com/watch?v=bwuajJlVgGs

Ivanka Trump speaks at the Skift Global Forum, the largest creative business forum in the global travel industry, about the importance of obsessing over the details.

Ivanka Trump's Remarks at the Fortune Most Powerful Women Summit
http://time.com/4537020/ivanka-trump-fortune-women-summit

Ivanka Trump, daughter of Republican presidential nominee Donald Trump, sat down with *Time*'s Nancy Gibbs for an interview at *Fortune* magazine's Most Powerful Women Summit in Dana Point, California.

BIBLIOGRAPHY

Abrams, Rachel. "Despite a Trust, Ivanka Trump Still Wields Power Over Her Brand." *New York Times*, March 20, 2017. https://www.nytimes.com/2017/03/20/business/despite-trust-ivanka-trump-still-wields-power-over-her-brand.html.

Agness, Karin. "Five Under-40 Women at the GOP Convention Share the Surprising Reasons They're Voting for Trump." *Forbes*, July 21, 2016. http://www.forbes.com/sites/karinagness/2016/07/21/this-is-what-women-delegates-think-of-trump/#1f965d605207.

Agovino, Theresa. "Javanka! Real Estate's Newlyweds." *Crain's New York Business*, November 15, 2009. http://www.crainsnewyork.com/article/20091115/FREE/311159973/javanka-real-estates-newlyweds.

Barbaro, Michael, and Jonathan Mahler. "Quiet Fixer in Donald Trump's Campaign: His Son-in-Law, Jared Kushner." *New York Times*, July 4, 2016. https://www.nytimes.com/2016/07/05/us/politics/jared-kushner-donald-trump.html.

Bertoni, Steven. "Exclusive Interview: How Jared Kushner Won Trump the White House. *Forbes*, December 20, 2016. http://www.forbes.com/sites/stevenbertoni/2016/11/22/exclusive-interview-how-jared-kushner-won-trump-the-white-house/#106f5fa22f50.

Blair, Gwenda. *The Trumps: Three Generations That Built an Empire*. New York: Simon and Schuster, 2009.

Braley, Sarah J. F. "Trump Collection Set to Exceed 30 Hotels by 2020: Ivanka Trump Reflects on Brand's Unique

Positioning." *Meetings & Conventions*, July 2014. http://go.galegroup.com/ps/i.do?p=ITOF&sw=w&u=nysl_we_becpl&v=2.1&it=r&id=GALE%7CA377861905&asid=ab7d5a00b081829f9d54998d80a4a43f.

Chabbott, Sophia. "Ivanka Trump Sets Aggressive Goals, Naturally." *Women's Wear Daily*, February 1, 2010. http://go.galegroup.com/ps/i.do?p=ITOF&sw=w&u=nysl_we_becpl&v=2.1&it=r&id=GALE%7CA221753198&asid=8ed97dd5e572d00aa0c245d088e7c9bd.

Dangremond, Sam. "Ivanka Trump's Park Avenue 'Starter' Apartment Is for Sale." *Town & Country*, December 15, 2016. http://www.townandcountrymag.com/leisure/real-estate/g3124/ivanka-trump-park-avenue-apartment-for-sale.

DePaulo, Lisa. "Ivanka Trump's Plan for Total World Domination." *GQ*, April 12, 2007. http://www.gq.com/story/ivanka-trump.

Dullea, Georgia. "At Work With: Ivana Trump; Thinner, Blonder, Wiser." *New York Times*, April 5, 1995. http://www.nytimes.com/1995/04/05/garden/at-work-with-ivana-trump-thinner-blonder-wiser.html?pagewanted=all.

Eris, Alfred. "Some Get Rich, Some Don't." *Popular Mechanics*, March 1951.

Flegenheimer, Matt, Rachel Abrams, Barry Meier, and Hiroko Tabucchi. "Business Since Birth: Trump's Children and the Tangle that Awaits." *New York Times*, December 4, 2016. http://www.nytimes.com/2016/12/04/us/politics/trump-family-ivanka-donald-jr.html?_r=0.

Glowczewska, Klara. "I Took a Behind-the-Scenes Tour of the New Trump Hotel in Washington DC." *Town & Country*, September 9, 2016. http://www.townandcountrymag.com/leisure/travel-guide/news/a7784/trump-hotel-washington-dc-opening.

Grove, Lloyd. "Ivanka Trump." *Entrepreneur*, November 10, 2008. https://www.entrepreneur.com/article/198386.

Haberman, Maggie, and Jo Becker. "Donald Trump Is Said to Intend to Keep a Stake in His Business." *New York Times*, December 7, 2016. https://www.nytimes.com/2016/12/07/us/politics/trump-organization-ivanka-trump.html.

Haberman, Maggie, and Rachel Abrams. "Ivanka Trump, Shifting Plans, Will Become a Federal Employee." *New York Times*, March 29, 2017. https://www.nytimes.com/2017/03/29/us/politics/ivanka-trump-federal-employee-white-house.html?smid=tw-share&_r=0&utm_source=huffingtonpost.com&utm_medium=referral&utm_campaign=pubexchange_article.

Haight, Sarah. "Ivanka Trump, Mogul: Fashion Line Grows, but Is She For Real?" *Women's Wear Daily*, August 3, 2010. http://go.galegroup.com/ps/i.do?p=ITOF&sw=w&u=nysl_we_becpl&v=2.1&it=r&id=GALE%7CA234162854&asid=36e73a244a972e68d74e99d3344b1359.

Heney, Paul J. "Ivanka Trump Keeps Hotels Contextual." *Hotel & Motel Management*, October 5, 2009. http://go.galegroup.com/ps/i.do?p=ITOF&sw=w&u=nysl_we_becpl&v=2.1&it=r&id=GALE%7CA212412711&asid=ddf51d0536f5fdbe97964f510acd19bd.

Herbst, Kendall. "Ivanka Trump Talks Gossip Girl Cameo." *InStyle*, October 27, 2010. http://www.instyle.com/news/ivanka-trump-talks-gossip-girl-cameo.

Hoang, Paul. "Ivanka Trump: Paul Hoang Profiles the Highly Successful American Businesswoman, Fashion Model and Heiress." *Business Review*, November 2010. http://go.galegroup.com/ps/i.do?p=ITOF&sw=w&u=nysl_we_becpl&v=2.1&it=r&id=GALE%7CA241529534&asid=391470048b61e9176fa29817cb915890.

Hu, Hui-Yong, and Blake Schmidt. "Trump's Hotel Company Takes Name Off Rio de Janeiro Property." *Bloomberg*, December 13, 2016. https://www.bloomberg.com/news/articles/2016-12-14/trump-s-hotel-company-takes-name-off-rio-de-janeiro-property.

Hyland, Véronique. "A Registered Democrat Is Currently Running Ivanka Trump's Brand." *Cut*, March 7, 2017. http://nymag.com/thecut/2017/03/abigail-klem-takes-over-as-president-of-ivanka-trumps-brand.html.

Iggulden, Caroline. "Donald's Trump Card: Who Is Ivanka Trump? Meet the Real First Lady and Possibly the Reason Donald Trump Won the US Election." *Sun*, November 11, 2016. https://www.thesun.co.uk/news/2161436/ivanka-trump-first-lady-donald-us-election-2016.

Itzkoff, Dave. "Reluctant Apprentices." *New York Times*, December 31, 2006. http://www.nytimes.com/2006/12/31/arts/television/31itzk.html.

Johnson, Jamie. "Born Rich Inside Ivanka's Childhood Bedroom." HBO, 2003. Posted October 22, 2013. https://www.youtube.com/watch?v=RJ_51359FIs.

Karni, Annie. "Ivanka Trump Set to Get West Wing Office as Role Expands." *Politico*, March 20, 2017. http://www.politico.com/story/2017/03/ivanka-trump-white-house-236273.

———. "Ivanka Trump Turns to Goldman Sachs Partner for Advice." *Politico*, January 5, 2017. http://www.politico.com/story/2017/01/ivanka-trump-goldman-sachs-233234.

La Ferla, Ruth. "Introducing the Ivanka." *New York Times*, December 27, 2007. http://www.nytimes.com/2007/12/27/fashion/27IVANKA.html.

Lockwood, Lisa. "Ivanka Trump in Deal for Home Collection." *Women's Wear Daily*, February 1, 2013. http://go.galegroup.com/ps/i.do?p=ITOF&sw=w&u=nysl_we_becpl&v=2.1&it=r&id=GALE%7CA318281845&asid=6f576c72cf65ecd052959fb23f617d78.

Mahler, Jonathan. "In Campaign and Company, Ivanka Trump Has a Central Role." *New York Times*, April 16, 2016. https://www.nytimes.com/2016/04/17/us/politics/ivanka-trump-donald-trump.html?_r=0.

Moin, David. "Ivanka Trump Plays Another Card." *Women's Wear Daily*, March 28, 2012. http://go.galegroup.com/ps/i.do?p=ITOF&sw=w&u=nysl_we_becpl&v=2.1&it=r&id=GALE%7CA285340980&asid=65a9f27fe1d9efce11a3dd2212e4b53e.

"Movers and Shakers." *Vogue*, January 2008. http://go.galegroup.com/ps/i.do?p=ITOF&sw=w&u=nysl_we_becpl&v=2.1&it=r&id=GALE%7CA177657587&asid=e136948a6736b2153fa8197f947763d2.

Mullany, Anjali. "Consumer 'Interest' in Ivanka Trump's Brand Has Fallen Since the Boycott Began." *Fast Company*, November 14, 2016. https://www.fastcompany.com/3065651/election-2016/consumer-interest-in-ivanka-trumps-brand-has-fallen-since-the-boycott-began.

———. "Ivanka Trump Doesn't Flinch." *Fast Company*, October 17, 2016. https://www.fastcompany.com/3063963/behind-the-brand/ivanka-trump-doest-flinch.

Peters, Jeremy W. "Citizen Kushner." *New York Times*, June 24, 2011. http://www.nytimes.com/2011/06/26/fashion/life-in-the-fishbowl-for-jared-kushner.html.

Robehmed, Natalie. "Ivanka Trump on Being the Other Trump." *Forbes*, May 16, 2016. http://www.forbes.com/sites/natalierobehmed/2016/05/12/being-the-other-trump-ivanka-trumps-mission-for-success-despite-her-dad/#285480a6ff60.

Shattuck, Kathryn. "What's On Tonight." *New York Times*, January 3, 2008. http://query.nytimes.com/gst/fullpage.html?res=9407E5DF1539F930A35752C0A96E9C8B63.

Stanley, Alessandra, and Jacob Bernstein. "Will Ivanka Trump Be the Most Powerful First Daughter in History?" *New York Times*, December 3, 2016. http://www.nytimes.com/2016/12/03/fashion/ivanka-trump-first-daughter.html?action=click&contentCollection=Politics&module=RelatedCoverage®ion=Marginalia&pgtype=article.

Strugatz, Rachel. "Ivanka Trump Line Goes Green." *Women's Wear Daily*, June 6, 2011. http://go.galegroup.com/ps/i.do?p=ITOF&sw=w&u=nysl_we_becpl&v=2.1&it=r&id=GALE%7CA258917199&asid=edefefa9c553085049742301bc0085df.

Teeman, Tim. "Ivanka Trump Talks Being a Mogul, a Mother, and More." *Town & Country*, October 19, 2016. http://www.townandcountrymag.com/society/money-and-power/a4616/ivanka-trump-2016.

———. "Trump Card." *Town & Country*, February 2016. http://go.galegroup.com/ps/i.do?p=ITOF&sw=w&u=nysl_we_becpl&v=2.1&it=r&id=GALE%7CA441490882&asid=fc5a4e984892ea46e8328a41db491750.

Traister, Rebecca. "Ivanka Is Right About Promoting Gender Equality—and Her Father Will Do the Exact Opposite." *New York Magazine*, July 22, 2016. http://nymag.com/thecut/2016/07/ivanka-trump-rnc-speech-wrong.html.

Triggs, Charlotte. "Inside Ivanka Trump's Chaotic Life Raising Three Children with Husband Jared Kushner: 'I'm Exhausted 90 Percent of the Time.'" *People*, July 21, 2016. http://celebritybabies.people.com/2016/07/21/ivanka-trump-raising-three-children-jared-kushner-exhausted.

Trump, Ivana. *The Best Is Yet to Come: Coping With Divorce and Enjoying Life Again*. New York: Simon and Schuster, 1995.

Trump, Ivanka. *The Trump Card: Playing to Win in Work and Life*. New York: Simon and Schuster, 2009.

———. "2016 Republican National Convention Speech." Delivered July 21, 2016, Cleveland, OH. https://www.youtube.com/watch?v=0JdxeWyL8VU.

Van Meter, Jonathan. "Ivanka Trump Knows What It Means to Be a Modern Millennial." *Vogue*, February 25, 2015. http://www.vogue.com/11739787/ivanka-trump-collection-the-apprentice-family.

Walden, Celia. "Donald Trump's Daughter Ivanka: Why I Watch My Baby on CCTV." *Telegraph*, June 11, 2012. http://www.telegraph.co.uk/women/mother-tongue/9323013/Donald-Trumps-daughter-Ivanka-Why-I-watch-my-baby-on-CCTV.html.

Ward, Kristina Stewart. "Daddy's Little Girl: She May Be Donald's Daughter, but Make No Mistake: Ivanka Trump Is Her Own Woman." *Town & Country*, July 2008. http://go.galegroup.com/ps/i.do?p=ITOF&sw=w&u=nysl_we_becpl&v=2.1&it=r&id=GALE%7CA182524809&asid=4e93fb90d1acdf5b7637cb11cb9ada08.

Wead, Doug. *All the Presidents' Children: Triumph and Tragedy in the Lives of America's First Families*. New York: Atria Books, 2003.

White, Daniel, Katie Reilly, and Melissa Chan. "Read Ivanka Trump's Remarks at the Fortune Most Powerful Women Summit." *Time*, October 19, 2016. http://time.com/4537020/ivanka-trump-fortune-women-summit.

Widdicombe, Lizzie. "Ivanka and Jared's Power Play." *New Yorker*, August 22, 2016. http://www.newyorker.com/magazine/2016/08/22/ivanka-trump-and-jared-kushners-power-play.

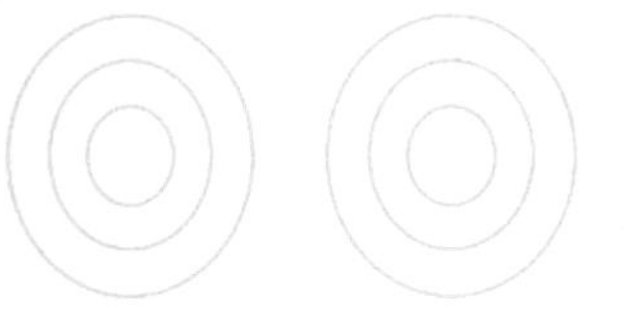

INDEX

Page numbers in **boldface** are illustrations. Entries in **boldface** are glossary terms.

ABOUT THE AUTHOR

Megan Mills Hoffman grew up in the Alaskan wilderness only reading about New York fashion, politics, and culture. She set out to craft her own entrepreneurial dreams of living life more daringly by exploring different versions of story making and social movements across the country. With a bachelor's in sociology, she studies the way people learn and how we navigate complex problems in today's global society. She now lives in Buffalo, New York, with her husband and daughter, who make it possible for her to write. This is her second title for Cavendish Square, her first being about a very different sort of international conqueror, Napoleon Bonaparte.